MinnowKnits, 100

MinnowKnits™, Too

More Uncommon Knits for Kids, Big and Small

JIL EATON

A MinnowKnits™ Book

PHOTOGRAPHS BY NINA FULLER

Clarkson Potter/Publishers
New York

Every effort has been made to be accurate and complete with all
the information in this book. The publisher and the author
cannot, however, be responsible for differences in knitters' abili-
ties, techniques, tools, or conditions, or any resulting damages
or mistakes or losses.

MinnowKnits™ hand-knitting patterns may not be knit for resale. For more
information on Jil Eaton and MinnowKnits™, write to us at Small
Pond Studios, 52 Neal Street, Portland, ME 04102, USA.

Published by Clarkson N. Potter/Publishers, New York, New York
Member of the Crown Publishing Group, a division of Random
House, Inc.
www.crownpublishing.com

CLARKSON N. POTTER, is a trademark and POTTER and
colophon are registered trademarks of Random House, Inc.

Originally published in hardcover in the United States by Clarkson
Potter/Publishers, a division of Random House, Inc., in 1998.

Printed in China

TECHNICAL WRITING AND EDITING: Carla Scott
PATTERN CHECKING: Mary Milam
KNITTING: Mary Milam, Mary Merrill, Nita Young, Audrey Lewis,
Carlyn Gilbert, and Leslie Scanlon
ART DIRECTION: Jil Eaton (for photography)
STYLING: Merle Hagelin, Isabel Smiles, Jil Eaton
PHOTOGRAPHY: Nina Fuller
ILLUSTRATIONS: Jil Eaton
LEARN-TO-KNIT ILLUSTRATIONS: Joni Coniglio
DESIGN: Susan DeStaebler
PRODUCTION: Joy Sikorski

Library of Congress Cataloging-in-Publication Data
Eaton, Jil
    MinnowKnits™, too: more uncommon knits for kids, big and
small / Jil Eaton. — 1st ed.
    1. Knitting—Patterns.   2. Children's clothing.   I. Title.
TT825.E285   1998
746.43'20432—dc21   97-15495

ISBN 1-4000-5248-3

10 9 8 7 6 5 4 3 2 1

FIRST PAPERBACK EDITION

For You Two

■ This book is dedicated to my husband, David, and to my son, Alexander, who waited for dinner, put off trips and outings, rearranged schedules, endured endless photo shoots and knitting emergencies, dragged around props, greeted anxious mothers wrangling wailing babies at the break of dawn in the living room, and generally put up with me during this wild and wooly year; all in all two of the most extraordinary, patient, supportive, funny, kind, understanding, and loving beings on the planet!

Contents

Autumn   89

Winter   121

Preface

■ 1954. The year the snow blew great drifts higher than the signs on my father's store. The year my ducks got loose and waddled through town, stopping traffic all the way to the Sandy River. The year I fell in love with David Etzel, and he gave me a fishing rod for my birthday. The year I turned five, and learned to knit.

Time flies, but I remember it so very clearly. What magic! My young and beautiful mother, curled with me on the corner of our huge down-filled couch in front of the fire. Knit one, purl two. Just two sticks and a string, and voilà! Recently my mother found my old dolls' trunk in her barn. Papered with labels from exotic foreign countries, it was full of my early original knitwear. Using odds and ends from the knitting basket, I had fashioned all sorts of outfits. Hats, sweaters, pantaloons, tea dresses—even an eight-sleeved sweater for my stuffed octopus! Colors rioted together, stitches were lost here and there, but the ensemble was charming.

Little did I know then that so many years later I would be creating hand-knitting patterns for children's wear for knitters all over the world.

I am now a design professional, and color and shape are still the most important elements for me, in garments that are quick to knit but still full of style, charm, and wit. I apply sophisticated ideas and design principles to simple-to-make-and-wear yet uncommon outfits for children.

Because I know the pleasure of watching a garment magically form on two sticks, I hope you will always keep your basket full of rich and brilliant yarns for your own wonderful knitting projects. We all may be wildly busy with our full and varied lives, but knitting remains a time to be still, to dream and create.

Remember, when we are knitting, all is right with the world!

Jil Eaton

Portland, Maine
February 1998

Introduction

■ In this season-by-season collection, children celebrate holidays and birthdays, enjoy spirited shenanigans, or simply play in the snow. The twenty-six festive patterns presented here place hand-knits firmly in our daily lives. Hand-knits are durable, comfortable clothes that become precious hand-me-downs! Children, aged three months to eight years, romp through the year clad in sweaters, hats, dresses, vests, coats, snowsuits, and pantaloons in delightful colors and designs.

Throughout this book I have sprinkled my personal tips and hints to make your work technically simple while more beautifully crafted, enjoyable, and polished. Also you will find complete instructions for learning to knit, with drawings for casting-on, knitting, purling, decreasing, and binding off—everything you need to know. All patterns are photographed on location in the everyday world, as well as in the studio, to give you a clear and workable portrait of the garment.

Schematics with all measurements are provided for each garment, and I will keep reminding you to *always measure your child!* I have worked on developing my pattern templates for years, resulting in garments that are as easy to wear as they are to knit. Arm and neck openings are generous; silhouettes are easy and full, and generally the sizing is more ample than often found in knitting patterns. It is simple to adjust your work to fit your own child, and as far as I can tell, children come in wildly various sizes and shapes, some tall and lanky, others with short, stocky trunks and chubby extremities. I have formulated sizing somewhere in the middle, erring graciously to comfort and ease. After measuring your child, *round up* to the closest pattern size. Although these patterns are quick to knit, hand-knitting does take time, and we have found that children grow at an alarming rate! Once we carefully measured a model, only to find she had grown out of the garment by the time of the photo shoot three months later.

Getting Started:
Tips & Technicalities

■ Gauge

Gauge . . . gauge . . . gauge! Gauge is one of the most important aspects of a successful knitting project, and as my students know, I am always saying, "But what's your gauge? Where's your gauge swatch? Are you getting your gauge?" Somehow, when I learned to knit at age five, I missed the part about gauge, and it wasn't until I was in college that I took a class and learned the gauge lesson once and for all. If you are not getting the correct gauge, that is, *the correct number of stitches per inch/centimeter,* and the correct number of rows, the results of your knitting will be wildly variable. If you are even a half stitch off your gauge, the effect is significant. For instance, if your required gauge is 5 stitches to the inch, and you are getting 5.5, your 20-inch size 2 sweater will be 22 inches. Worse still, if you are getting 4.5 stitches to the inch, you will end up with a circumference of 18 inches, which might not go around your child. Not only that, but too few stitches per inch make a tension that is too loose; too many make a fabric with a tight tension. Different needles of the same size

can make a big difference, too, so always do your swatch on the needles you will actually be using to make the garment. No matter how consistent a knitter you think you are, always make a gauge stitch. The time you spend will save you time in the long run. If you want your garments to fit, if you want your handwork to be perfect—just do your swatch!

■ Swatch

Using the needles and yarn recommended in the pattern, cast on the correct number of stitches to make a 4-inch/10-centimeter piece, plus 6 stitches. Work 3 rows in garter stitch, and then begin the pattern, always working 3 stitches at the beginning of every row in garter. Work until the swatch measures 4 inches, work 3 more rows of garter, and bind off evenly. Stretch your swatch gently in all directions, and lay it on a hard, flat surface. Measuring inside the garter stitch rows, you should have 4 inches/10 centimeters exactly. If your swatch is too big, go down a needle size; if it's too small, up a size. Keep working until you achieve the correct gauge.

■ Count Rows

I often include instructions for row counting in the pattern text, and you can always count your rows based on the chart for each garment. If you count rows, garment pieces will always be a perfect match, for lovely results. A back that has been stretched to match a front will always bother you later. One easy technique is to thread a contrasting colored yarn up the front of the work, catching it in as if carrying color every 2 inches. I leave those strands in until the garment is almost ready to wear, for quick and easy counting and measuring. This trick makes fitting a snap!

■ Sizing

Always measure your child. It is very simple to alter a pattern, making sleeves longer or shorter, making dresses or pants specific lengths to fit your own child. (Always make adjustments in the lower section of leggings or sleeves.) Just remember that you may need a bit more yarn if your child is long-limbed. The template I have developed over the years is comfortable for kids, easy for parents for dressing, and just plain wearable. I have found many children's patterns to have stingy neck and arm openings, and have accommodated a generous measure of ease in my sizing. It might also help you to measure a garment that fits your child loosely now; even though many of my patterns are QuickKnits™ (any patterns with the QuickKnit™ mark are quick and easy to knit, perfect for beginners or busy knitters), it does take a bit of time to knit anything, and kids grow like weeds!

■ Measure Up!

The following will help you measure your child, which along with *getting your gauge* will be a giant step toward a garment that fits perfectly.

A. For hats, measure the widest part of the head, just above the ears.

B. This measurement is called CBS, or center-back-sleeve. Measure from the middle of the back straight across to the wrist. This figure will tell you how to adjust the sleeve length, no matter what the design.

C. The chest measurement is probably the most important. Measure around the chest about 1 inch down from the arm. You might also want to measure a garment that fits your child comfortably around the chest as well, to aid in finding the correct size.

D. Waist measurements are important for pantaloons, for adjusting the elastic.

E. Shoulder-to-waist shows the torso length, useful for adjustments in overall garment length.

F. For tunics or longer sweaters, knowing this measurement lets you knit the garment accordingly.

G. By adding F and G you will know the correct length for pantaloons.

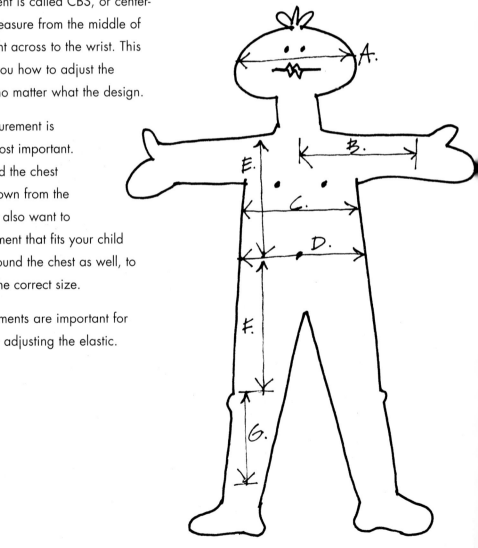

■ The Right Stuff

I use the most beautiful yarns I can find, and I believe you should always honor your handwork with the best in materials. I love wool for its warmth, elasticity, durability, and ability to hold beautiful dyes. The new cotton yarns are also excellent, holding their shape and color. Cotton breathes, and is comfortable in a great range of weather and climates. It is flame resistant and durable, perfect for children's wear.

My patterns are always generic, with the needed amounts for every garment given in yards and meters. You can substitute yarn colors and weights by doing just a bit of math, and yarn shops will always offer assistance for the math-impaired. I give the yarns that I have used for each knitted sample, so you can find the exact colors and weights; you also might want to experiment, choosing your own creative palette. But *always* use the very best yarns you can afford, in natural fibers and blends. Yarns today are wonderful, washable and durable, just the thing for heirlooms.

Those amazing turbos . . . I am always looking for the best materials and tools. Last year I discovered Addi Turbo circular knitting needles. They are billed as the "amazing turbos," which is perfectly accurate! Made of nickel-plated brass that is easy in your hands, soft and quiet, Addi Turbo needles actually speed up your knitting time. The soft cords let stitches glide quickly along the needles, without snags or catches to slow you down. I use the Addi circulars almost exclusively, simply working back and forth rather than around when appropriate. Addi Turbo circulars are sized from 12 to 60 inches, from US 000 to 36 in size, easily accommodating any project. Give them a try, and be amazed!

■ Schematics

The garment can be knit just from the schematic, with limited reference to the written instructions. I find knitting from schematics to be easier than trying to keep your place in complex and wordy instructions. French and Japanese patterns often have wonderful schematics, and we can knit from those without translations! As the world becomes smaller, perhaps we will achieve a universal system. Meanwhile, you can always refer to the schematic to check your knitting, and working with the schematics may very well

answer questions and solve problems for you. If you are altering a pattern for a specific child, it is helpful to make your own schematic on graph paper.

■ A Note on Instruction Abbreviations

Here are a few examples of how to read the shaping in the schematics: 1×4 (5, 6), 2×3, 1×2 means bind off from shaped edge 4 (or 5 or 6, depending on size) stitches once, 3 stitches twice, 2 stitches once. P/u means pick up. Another example is -2/2x, -1/3x, which means decrease 2 stitches every other row twice, then decrease 1 stitch every other row 3 times. Unless stated, the shaping is worked every other row. For example, -1/4r's/9x, -1/6r's/5x means decrease 1 stitch every 4th row 9 times, every 6th row 5 times. The shaping is written for one side only. If there is shaping on both sides, such as on the armhole or sleeve edge, be sure to decrease on both sides. If you are unsure about the shaping, look at the schematic to find the shape or refer back to the written instructions. Knitting with the help of these schematics will simplify your work in the end. Or try knitting from just a schematic as the French or the Japanese do; once you do, you'll be hooked!

■ Show Your Colors

I find many knitters to be skittish about color-work, but using more than one color adds style and dash to a garment. The colorwork I do may look complex, with its rich results, but generally I work with only two colors at a time. Working in two-stranded colors for details or edges adds a lot of verve with a little bit of effort. So do give colorwork a try—I think you'll be happily surprised!

Color charts are included for patterns with multistranded knitting. Work the charts from the bottom up, and from right to left. The color charts show the place-ment of various colors as they will appear on the right

side of the fabric. *Jacquard* is the term we use for any stranded two-color knitting, and is worked in either Fair Isle or intarsia methods.

Fair Isle is technically done in the round, but can be done on two needles if preferred. Fair Isle is used for geometrics, diamonds, snowflakes, and overall dot patterning. The color not being worked is carried, or stranded, behind the knitting. Never carry over more than two or three stitches, or the result will be an uneven tension. A long carryover or float not only ruins the tension but produces a fabric that is easily snagged as it is put on and taken off the child. Carry your colors up the edge by catching them in every few rows. Make sure you do not pull the yarn that is being carried too tight, for this will distort the fabric. The most daunting thing about two-color knitting is learning to maintain an even tension; think loose and smooth.

Intarsia is used for large areas of color that are worked vertically as well as horizontally. Wind the colors being used on separate bobbins, which are available at yarn shops. After working the stitches for the first color, join the second color and twist it around the first color strand in order to eliminate the holes that would otherwise appear. After switching to the next color, cut the yarn and set the bobbin aside. In intarsia, the yarn is not carried behind the work.

■ Finishing, Blocking, and Laundering

Finish in the morning, in good light, on a flat surface. Finishing the knitting is one thing, but finishing the actual garment is another complete task, requiring rested concentration and attention to detail. It is always so tempting to quickly sew up a garment the minute it is off the needles, but good finishing can mean the difference between a beautiful piece and a mediocre effort, so wait until you're fresh and able. Tip:

When you are adding colors or the next ball of yarn, leave a 6-inch length, which will make the weaving in at the end much easier.

When your knitting is complete, weave in all the loose tails of yarn on each piece. Cover each piece with two damp towels, one under and one over, pinning the pieces in place. Using a steam iron, lightly press at the appropriate setting; then dry flat on a towel, on a rack if you have one. Blocking improves the look of the garment, as long as it is gently done, without mashing down the fibers. Be gentle.

When it comes time to launder a garment for the first time, gauge swatches come in very handy for testing washability, following the yarn label instructions. I also find many yarns are machine washable, if you put them on a very gentle and cool cycle in a small mesh bag, which gets them really clean. Dry garments flat, gently reblocking them on a terry towel, and let them air-dry on a rack if possible.

If you take good care of your hand-knits, they will take care of you for many years!

Learn to Knit

The following learn-to-knit instructions take you through the basic elements of knitting. The first step is the slip knot, followed by two types of cast-ons, the "Knit-on Cast-on" and the "Cable Cast-on." The cast-on gets the loops of yarn started onto the needles. Once you have learned the knit-on method, you have actually learned the basic knit stitch. The cable cast-on is a variation of the first method, and is used to form a sturdier, yet elastic, edge.

■ Slip Knot

1. Hold the yarn in the left hand, leaving a short length free. Wrap the yarn from the skein into a circle and bring the yarn from below and up through the center of the circle. Insert the needle under this strand as shown.

2. Pull on both the short and long ends to tighten the knot on the needle.

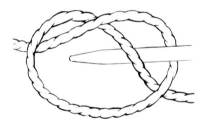

■ Knit-on Cast-on

1. Hold the needle with the slip knot in the left hand and the empty needle in the right hand. Insert the right needle from front to back under the left needle and through the stitch. With the yarn in the right hand, wrap the yarn around the right needle as shown.

2. With the tip of the right needle, pull the wrap through the stitch on the left needle and bring to the front.

3. Slip the new stitch off the left needle and onto the right needle.

   Repeat steps 1 to 3 until you have the necessary number of stitches for the row.

■ Cable Cast-on

1. Follow steps 2 and 3 for the Knit-on Cast-on (above).

2. Insert the right needle between the first two stitches on the left needle and wrap the yarn around the needle as shown. Repeat until you have the necessary number of stitches for the row.

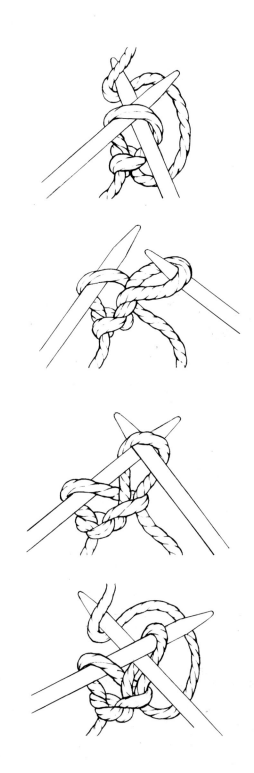

■ Basic Knit Stitch

The knit stitch is the simplest of all knitting techniques and is the basis for everything else you will learn. Rows knitted back to back are called the garter stitch.

1. Hold the needle with the cast-on stitches in the left hand and hold the empty needle in the right hand. Insert the right needle from front to back into the first stitch on the left needle and wrap the yarn as you did in step 1 of the cast-on.

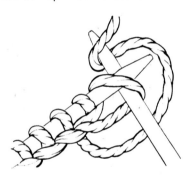

2. With the tip of the right needle, pull the wrap through the stitch on the left needle and onto the right needle. Drop the stitch from the left needle as the new stitch is

made on the right needle. Repeat steps 1 and 2 until all the stitches from the left needle are on the right needle. Turn the work and hold the needle with the new stitches in the left hand and continue knitting back and forth.

■ Basic Purl Stitch

The purl stitch is basically the opposite of the knit stitch. Instead of pulling the wrapped yarn toward you, you will push it through the back of the stitch. Because it is harder to see what you are doing, the purl stitch is a bit harder to learn than the knit stitch. When you knit one row, then purl one row, you create the stockinette stitch.

Hold the needle with the cast-on stitches in the left hand and hold the empty needle in the right hand. Insert the right needle from back to front into the first stitch on the left needle and wrap the yarn counterclockwise around the right needle as shown. With the tip of the right needle, pull the wrap through

the stitch on the left needle and onto the right needle as in the knit stitch. Drop the stitch from the left needle. A new stitch is made on the right needle. Continue in this way across the row.

■ Stockinette Stitch

On straight needles, knit on right side, purl on wrong side. On a circular needle, knit every row.

■ Garter Stitch

When on straight needles, knit every row. On a circular needle, knit one row, purl one row.

■ Knit 2 Together (K2tog), or Decrease

Hold the needle with the knitted fabric in the left hand and hold the empty needle in the right hand. Insert the right needle from front to back through the first two stitches on the left needle. Wrap the yarn and pull through

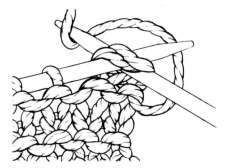

the two stitches as if knitting. Drop the two stitches from the left needle. One new stitch is made from two stitches, therefore one stitch is decreased.

■ Increase

The most common way to increase is to knit in the front of the stitch, and, without removing the stitch from the left-hand needle, knit in the back of the same stitch, then drop the stitch from the left-hand needle. This makes two stitches in one stitch.

■ Bind Off

Hold the needle with the knitting in the left hand and the empty needle in the right hand. Knit the first two stitches. *With the left needle in front of the right needle, insert the tip of the left needle into the second stitch on the right needle and pull it over the first stitch and off the right needle. One stitch has been bound off. Knit the next stitch, then repeat from * until all the stitches are bound off.

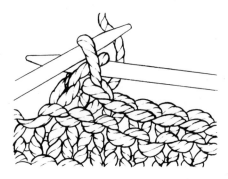

Learn-to-Knit Puppet

A perfect first QuickKnit™ knitting project is this adorable snake puppet. It is made using the knit stitch on both the front and the back of the work, a combination called the garter stitch. The puppet is perfect for beginners because it is an easy way to master knitting before going on to the more advanced stitches. There is simple shaping in this pattern, so you will learn how to decrease a stitch by knitting two stitches together (K2tog). And finally, you will learn how to bind off, which is necessary to complete any project. By binding off, you fasten off all remaining stitches so that they will not unravel. After you have mastered the knit stitch, go on to the purl stitch, and you will be able to knit up a storm! Puppets make an out-of-the-ordinary baby shower gift, and kids are entranced. This pattern is also a great way to use up your leftovers . . . try one in stripes!

■ Materials

Worsted weight wool *that will obtain gauge given below*

200 yd/182 m

Needles size 8 US (6 UK, 5 mm), *or size needed to obtain gauge*

Polar fleece (7.5 × 5.5 in./19 × 14 cm scrap)

Two buttons (for eyes)

Sample in photograph knit in Rowan Magpie worsted weight wool #306 Peony.

■ Gauge

18 sts and 32 rows = 4 in./10 cm in garter stitch using size 8 needles

Always check gauge to save time and ensure correct yardage!

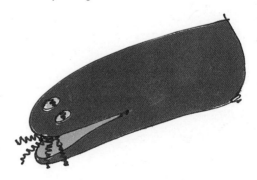

■ Body

Cast on 44 sts. Work in garter st (k every row) for 10 in./25.5 cm/80 rows.

Divide for Mouth: *Next row:* K22, place rem 22 sts on a holder (you can use a stitch holder, a large pin, or a short length of yarn). Cont on sts on needle for 1st half as foll: *Next row:* Knit. *Next row:* K2tog, k to last 2 sts on needle, k2tog. Rep last 2 rows (therefore 2 sts dec'd every other row) 6 times more. K 1 row even. Bind off rem 8 sts. Sl sts from holder to needle and work the 2nd half same as the 1st half.

■ Finishing

Fold puppet in half lengthwise and sew straight edge of side seam. Make mouth from fleece as shown in the diagram, and sew fleece along shaped sides of puppet to form mouth. Sew on buttons for eyes.

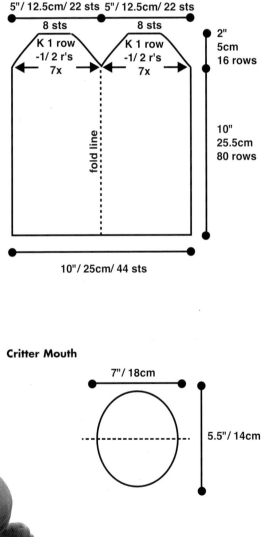

5"/ 12.5cm/ 22 sts   5"/ 12.5cm/ 22 sts

8 sts   8 sts

K 1 row -1/ 2 r's   7x   K 1 row -1/ 2 r's   7x

2" 5cm 16 rows

fold line

10" 25.5cm 80 rows

10"/ 25cm/ 44 sts

Critter Mouth

7"/ 18cm

5.5"/ 14cm

Spring

■ Spring is the time for birthing and daffodils, pussywillows and polliwogs. It's also the time to put away your wooly knitting and begin your spring projects in lightweight yarns. Dresses, coats, and waistcoats in fresh, bright colors are a treat to work on after the gray days of winter's end—for the bold chartreuse greens and sweet pea blues that remind us of new beginnings. At this time of year, children are happy and comfortable playing in soft cottons and airy wools, and cool cotton, durable and washable, is always one of the best fibers for children's wear. There are so many wonderful cottons available now, in vibrant, color-fast hues, that you'll find yourself easily inspired by this bunch of springtime patterns.

La Bébé

This simple cotton dress with zigzag hem and its matching bonnet with zigzag trim are very easy to knit once you finish the hem work, and the effect is charming. Small garter-stitch triangles are strung together on the needle and knit across to make the border treatment. I always weave in all the loose ends right away, making the project neater and easier to work. This dress is also darling in wool.

■ Sizes

3–6 Months

Dress finished chest (buttoned): 16 in./41 cm

Dress length, shoulder to hem: 26.25 in./66.5 cm

■ Materials

DK weight cotton that *will obtain gauge below*

Dress: 850 yd/765 m White

Bonnet: 140 yd/125 m White

Straight needles and double-pointed needles (dpn) sizes 4, 6 US (10, 8 UK; 3.5, 4 mm)

Circular needles sizes 5, 6 US (9, 8 UK; 3.75, 4 mm), 24 in./60 cm long, *or size needed to obtain gauge*

Crochet hook size F US (8 UK, 4 mm)

Six pearl half-round buttons, stitch holders, stitch markers, and .5 in./1.5 cm–wide satin ribbon for bonnet

■ Gauge

20 sts and 28 rows = 4 in./10 cm in St st using size 6 needles

Always check gauge to save time and ensure correct yardage and correct fit! Always measure your child!

Sample in photograph knit in Rowan DK Cotton #263 Bleached White.

DRESS

■ Zigzag hem

With size 6 straight needles cast on 2 sts. Work in garter st, inc 1 st at end of every row until there are 14 sts. Rep 12 more times, for a total of 13 triangles and 182 sts.

Place sts on larger circular needle. Join and place marker for beg of rnd. K 1 rnd, p 1 rnd, k 1 rnd. *K 3 rnds, p 3 rnds; rep from * twice more. Cont in St st until piece measures 20.5 in./52 cm above zigzag hem. Weave in ends of triangles.

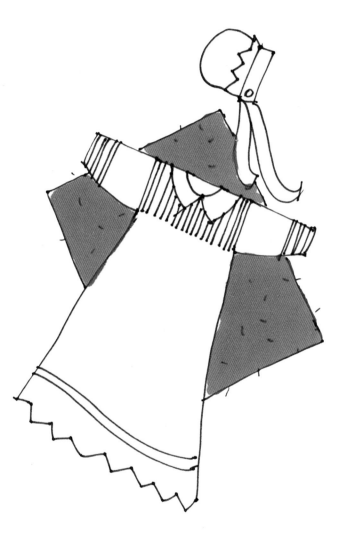

■ Bodice

Next rnd: K2tog around, to 91 sts. Change to size 4 dpn and work in k1, p1 rib for 2 rnds, dec 1 st on 1st rnd, to 90 sts.

Divide for front and back: With size 4 straight needles, work 45 sts for front, place rem sts on a holder for back. Working back and forth on front sts only, cont rib for 2.25 in./5.75 cm.

Neck shaping: Work 19 sts, join a 2nd skein of yarn and bind off center 7 sts for neck, work to end. Working both sides at same time, dec 1 st at each neck edge every other row 6 times, AT THE SAME TIME, when bodice measures 4 in./10 cm, work buttonholes on left side of front as foll: *Next (buttonhole) row:* Rib 1, yo (yarn over), k2tog, [rib 2, yo, k2tog] twice, rib to end. Work even until bodice measures 4.5 in./11.5 cm. Bind off left shoulder sts and place 13 sts of right shoulder on a holder.

■ Back

Work as for front, omitting neck shaping and buttonholes, and working last row as foll:
Next row (RS): Work 13 sts and place on a holder for right shoulder, bind off next 19 sts for neck, work to end. Cont on rem 13 sts in St st for left back button flap for 1 in./2.5 cm. Bind off.

Right shoulder seam: *With wrong sides facing each other,* place sts of back and front right shoulders on 2 parallel size 4 dpn. With a 3rd size 4 dpn, k through 1st st on each needle, then through the 2nd st on each needle, and pass 1st over 2nd to bind off. Cont in this way to end for a knitted seam.

■ Sleeves

Place markers on front and back 4 in./10 cm down from shoulder seams for armholes. With RS facing and size 6 dpn, pick up and k 40 sts between markers. Join and place marker at underarm. Work in St st (k every rnd) for 2.5 in./6.5 cm. Dec 1 st each end of next rnd (by knitting 2tog before and after marker), then every other rnd 6 times more, to 26 sts. P 3 rnds, k 3 rnds, p 3 rnds. Bind off purlwise.

■ Finishing

Collar: With RS facing and size 6 straight needles, beg at top of left front shoulder, pick up 52 sts evenly around neck edge. Work in k1, p1 rib for 2 rows, inc 5 sts evenly across last row, to 57 sts. Cont in garter st as foll:

Next row (WS): K40, join a 2nd skein of yarn and k17. Work both sides at same time for 16 rows more. Bind off. Make 3 button loops on left front collar edge. Sew buttons to shoulder and collar.

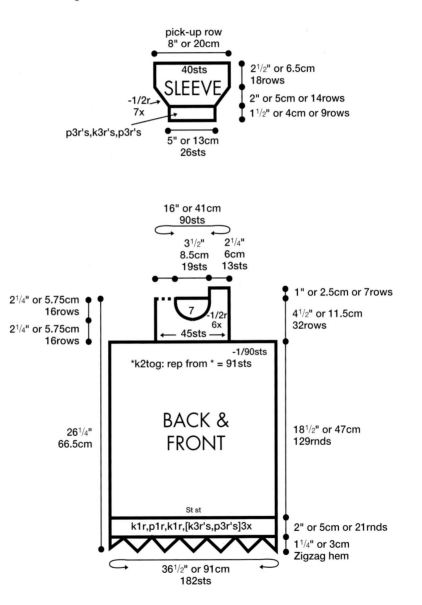

SLEEVE

pick-up row
8" or 20cm
40sts
2½" or 6.5cm
18rows
-1/2r→
7x
2" or 5cm or 14rows
1½" or 4cm or 9rows
p3r's,k3r's,p3r's
5" or 13cm
26sts

16" or 41cm
90sts
3½"
8.5cm
19sts
2¼"
6cm
13sts

2¼" or 5.75cm
16rows
2¼" or 5.75cm
16rows

7
-1/2r
6x
45sts

1" or 2.5cm or 7rows
4½" or 11.5cm
32rows

-1/90sts
*k2tog: rep from * = 91sts

BACK &
FRONT

26¼"
66.5cm

18½" or 47cm
129rnds

St st
k1r,p1r,k1r,[k3r's,p3r's]3x

2" or 5cm or 21rnds
1¼" or 3cm
Zigzag hem

36½" or 91cm
182sts

BONNET

With size 6 straight needles, cast on 19 sts for center panel. Work in St st (k on RS, p on WS) for 4.75 in./12 cm. Cut yarn. With RS facing and size 6 circular needle, pick up and k 24 sts along one side of center panel, work 19 sts of panel, pick up and k 24 sts along 2nd side of panel, to 67 sts. Cont in St st for 4.5 in./11.5 cm.

■ Ribbon facing

Change to size 5 circular needle. Work in rev St st (p on RS, k on WS) for .5 in./1.5 cm, end with a k row. K next row, dec 7 sts evenly across, to 60 sts. Work six 10-st triangles as foll: K10, turn work (leave rem sts unworked). *Next row:* *K2tog, k to end. Rep from * until 1 st rem. Fasten off. Work 5 more triangles in same way.

■ Finishing

Fold ribbon facing to RS of bonnet. With RS facing and crochet hook, work ch st edge through both thicknesses, along beg and ending row of ribbon facing. With RS facing and size 4 straight needles, pick and k 50 sts evenly along lower edge of bonnet, leaving openings of ribbon facing free. Work in k2, p2 rib for 1 in./2.5 cm. Bind off in rib. Weave a strand of yarn or elastic thread along lower edge of center panel above rib, pull to gather, adjusting to fit baby's head. Weave ribbon through facing and cut to desired length.

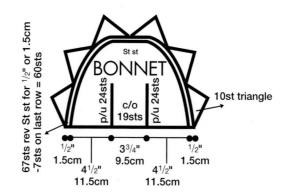

Spring Coat and Pillbox Hat

With the short French collar, ridged trim on the hem, and matching pillbox hat, this coat would have delighted Jackie O.! In DK cotton it is a QuickKnit™ and will work up prettily. The underarm pleats add ease as well as style to the garment. The Sweet Pea dress (page 61) is a perfect companion underneath.

■ Sizes

2 (4, 6) Years

Coat finished chest (buttoned): 22 (24, 27.5) in./54.5 (60.5, 68.5) cm

Coat length, shoulder to hem: 20 (21.5, 24.5) in./50.5 (55, 62) cm

Hat circumference: 17.5 (19, 20) in./44 (47, 50) cm

■ Materials

DK weight cotton *that will obtain gauge below*

Coat: 765 (1030, 1265) yd/690 (935, 1140) m Blue (MC)

Hat: 150 (165, 180) yd/135 (150, 165) m Blue (MC)

About 10 yd/9 m White (CC)

Needles sizes 5, 6 US (9, 8 UK; 3.75, 4 mm), *or size needed to obtain gauge*

Circular needles sizes 4, 6 US (10, 8 UK; 3.5, 4 mm), 29 in./74 cm long

One set (5) double-pointed needles (dpn) size 6 US (8 UK, 4 mm)

Crochet hook size E US (9 UK, 3.5 mm)

Three 5/8 in./1.5 cm buttons, stitch holders, and stitch markers

■ Gauge

20 sts and 28 rows = 4 in./10 cm in St st using larger needles

Always check gauge to save time and ensure correct yardage and correct fit! Always measure your child!

Sample in photograph knit in Rowan DK Cotton #217 Powder Blue (MC) and #263 Bleached White (CC).

COAT

■ Body

With larger circular needle and MC, cast on 226 (254, 286) sts. Work back and forth as with straight needles as foll: [P 1 row, k 1 row] twice, *[Next row (RS): Knit. Next row: K3, p to last 3 sts, k3] 3 times. [Next row (RS): K3, p to last 3 sts, k3. Next row: Knit.] twice*. Rep between *s once more.

Beg Gore: Next row (RS): K44 (49, 55), [sl 1 purlwise, k26 (30, 34), sl 1 purlwise, k27 (30, 34)] twice, sl 1 purlwise, k26 (30, 34), sl 1 purlwise, k44 (49, 55). Next row: K3, p to last 3 sts, k3. Rep last 2 rows for pat for 4 rows more. (Note: Cont to sl the slip sts purlwise on RS rows throughout.) Dec row (RS): K15 (16, 19), k3tog, work to last 18 (19, 22) sts, sl 1, k2tog, psso the k2tog (SK2P), k15 (16, 19). Rep dec row every 12th row 6 (7, 8) times more, AT THE SAME TIME, when piece measures 11.5 (12.5, 15) in./29 (32, 38) cm from beg, beg buttonholes. Buttonhole row (RS): K3, yo, k2tog, k to end. Rep buttonhole row every 3 in./7.5 cm twice more, AT THE SAME TIME, when piece measures 14 (15, 17) in./35.5 (38, 43) cm from beg, and there are 198 (222, 250) sts, work box pleats as foll: Next row (RS): K30 (33, 37), [bind off 28 (32, 36) sts (for pleat), k until there are 27 (30, 34) sts after pleat] twice, bind off 28 (32, 36) sts, k30 (33, 37). Next row: holding bound-off sts to p side of work, knit sts across to join, to 114 (126, 142) sts. Work even for 2 rows more.

Divide for front and back. Right front: K30 (33, 37), place rem 54 (60, 68) sts for back and 30 (33, 37) sts for left front on 2 holders to be worked later. Cont buttonholes on front, work until piece measures 18 (19, 21.5) in./ 45.75 (48.25, 54.5) cm from beg, end with a WS row.

Neck shaping: Next row (RS): Bind off 5 (7, 7) sts (neck edge), work to end. Cont to bind off from neck edge 3 sts twice, 2 sts once, and 1 st twice. When piece measures 20 (21.5, 24.5) in./51 (55, 62) cm from beg, place rem 15 (16, 20) sts on a holder for shoulder.

Back: Work as for right front, omitting neck shaping. Place first and last 15 (16, 20) sts on holders for shoulders and bind off rem 24 (28, 28) sts for neck.

Left front: Work to correspond to right front, reversing shaping.

Shoulder seams: With wrong sides facing, place sts of back and front right shoulders on 2 parallel dpn. With a 3rd dpn, k through 1st st on each needle, then through the 2nd st on each needle, and pass 1st over 2nd to bind off. Cont in this way to end for a knitted seam. Work in same way for left shoulder seam.

■ Sleeves

Place markers on front and back 5.5 (6, 7) in./14 (15, 17.5) cm down from shoulder seams for armholes. With RS facing and dpn, pick up and k 55 (60, 70) sts between markers. Join and place marker at underarm. Work in St st (k every rnd) for 4 rnds. Dec 1 st each end of next rnd (k2tog before and after marker), then every other rnd 2 (0, 0) times, every 4th rnd 8 (11, 14) times, to 33 (36, 40) sts. Work even until sleeve measures 6 (7.5, 9.5) in./15 (19, 24) cm. P 4 rnds, k 6 rnds, p 4 rnds. Bind off.

■ Finishing

Neckband: With RS facing and smaller straight needles, pick up and k 74 (82, 90) sts evenly around neck edge. K 1 row, (p 1 row, k 1 row) twice. Bind off.

Right front facing: With RS facing and crochet hook, beg at neck edge just below neckband, work sl st along inside of garter band to just above ridged border. Turn and working into front lps only, work *sc, skip 1 st, ch 1; rep from * to end. Work left front facing in same way, beg just above ridged border and ending at neck edge below neckband. Sew on buttons.

HAT

■ Top

With dpn, cast on 8 sts. Divide sts evenly over 4 needles (2 sts on each needle). Join and place marker for beg of rnd. K 1 rnd. *Next rnd:* Inc 1 st in each st, to 16 sts. K 3 rnds. *Next rnd:* Inc 1 st in each st, to 32 sts. K 5 rnds. *Next rnd:* Inc 1 st in each st, to 64 sts. K 7 rnds. *Next rnd for size 2 only:* [K1, inc 1 in next st] 32 times, to 96 sts. *Next rnd for size 4 only:* [K1, (inc 1 st in next st) twice, k1, inc 1 st in next st] 12 times, k1, inc 1 st

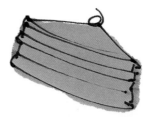

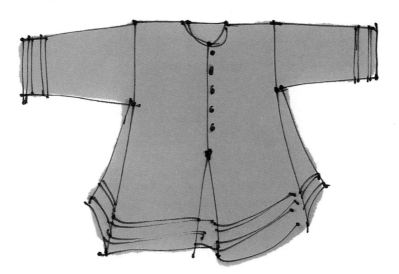

in next st, k1, to 102 sts. *Next rnd for size 6 only:* (Inc 1 st in next st) 3 times, [k1, (inc 1 in next st) twice] 20 times, inc 1 st in next st, to 108 sts. *For all sizes:* K 5 rnds.

■ Brim

P 3 rnds. K next rnd, dec 8 sts evenly around, to 88 (94, 100) sts. K 3 rnds. [P 3 rnds, k 4 rnds] twice.

■ Facing

Change to smaller circular needle, and p 1 rnd for turning ridge. Work in St st for 2.25 in./5.5 cm. Bind off. Fold facing to WS at turning ridge and sew in place.

■ Trim

With crochet hook and CC, work sl st in each loop of turning ridge. Fasten off.

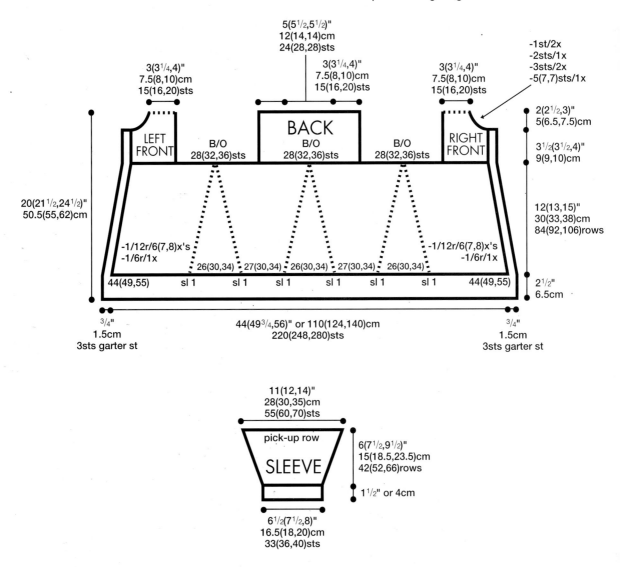

Bellissima

This day dress in double knitting cotton, an utterly plain QuickKnit™ except for the easy picot hems, is adorable with or without the sweet lace collar. I have found various ready-made collars in yard goods shops, but an heirloom lace collar would be enchanting. Or perhaps you could make your own!

■ Sizes

1 (2, 4, 6) Years

Finished chest (buttoned): 21 (23, 25, 27) in./52 (58, 62, 68) cm

Length, shoulder to hem: 20.5 (22, 24, 25.5) in./52 (55.5, 61, 64.5) cm

■ Materials

DK weight cotton *that will obtain gauge below*

765 (920, 1060, 1220) yd/690 (830, 955, 1100) m

Straight needles and double-pointed needles (dpn) size 6 US (8 UK, 4 mm), *or size needed to obtain gauge*

Circular needle size 6 US (8 UK, 4 mm), 16 in. or 24 in./40 cm or 60 cm long

Crochet hook size F (8 UK, 4 mm)

Lace collar, two .5 in./1.5 cm round buttons, stitch holders, and stitch markers

■ Gauge

20 sts and 28 rows = 4 in./10 cm in St st

Always check gauge to save time and ensure correct yardage and correct fit! Always measure your child!

Sample (from back) in photograph knit in Rowan DK Cotton #294 Royal.

■ Skirt

With circular needle, cast on 208 (232, 248, 272) sts. Join and place marker for beg of rnd. Work 6 rnds in St st. *Picot rnd:* *Yo, k2tog; rep from * around. Cont in St st until piece measures 15 (16, 17.5, 19) in./38 (40.5, 44.5, 48) cm from picot rnd. *Next rnd:* K2tog around, to 104 (116, 124, 136) sts. **Divide for front and back:** *Next rnd:* K52 (58, 62, 68) and place on a holder for back, k to end for front. Cont on straight needles.

■ Front Bodice

Work front sts back and forth in St st for 3.75 (4.25, 4.75, 4.75) in./9.5 (10.5, 12, 12) cm, ending with a WS row.
Neck shaping: Work 19 (22, 24, 27) sts, join a 2nd skein of yarn and bind off center 14 sts, work to end. Working both sides at the same time, dec 1 st at each neck edge every other row 4 times. Work even on rem 15 (18, 20, 23) sts each side until bodice measures 5.5 (6, 6.5, 6.5) in./14 (15, 16.5, 16.5) cm. Place sts on a holder for later finishing.

■ Back bodice

Work as for front, omitting neck shaping, until bodice measures 3 (3.5, 4, 4) in./7.5 (9, 10, 10) cm.
Divide for placket: Work 26 (29, 31, 34) sts, join a 2nd skein of yarn, and work to end. Work both sides at same time until same length as front. Bind off 11 sts from each neck edge, place rem 15 (18, 20, 23) sts on holders for shoulders.
Shoulder seams: *With wrong sides facing each other,* place sts of back and front right shoulders on 2 parallel dpn. With a 3rd dpn, k through 1st st on each needle, then through

the 2nd st on each needle, and pass 1st over 2nd to bind off. Cont in this way to end for a knitted seam. Work in same way for left shoulder seam.

■ Sleeves

Place markers on front and back 5.5 (6, 6.5, 6.5) in./14 (15, 16.5, 16.5) cm down from shoulder seams for armholes. With RS facing and dpn, pick up and k 56 (60, 66, 66) sts between markers. Join and place marker at underarm. Work in St st for 4.5 (5, 5, 5) in./11.5 (12.5, 12.5, 12.5) cm. Work picot rnd as on skirt. Work 6 rnds St st. Bind off loosely.

■ Finishing

Sew 2 buttons evenly along left back placket. With crochet hook, make chain button loops on right back placket, opposite buttons. Sew lace collar around neck. Fold hems in half to WS at picot rnd and sew in place.

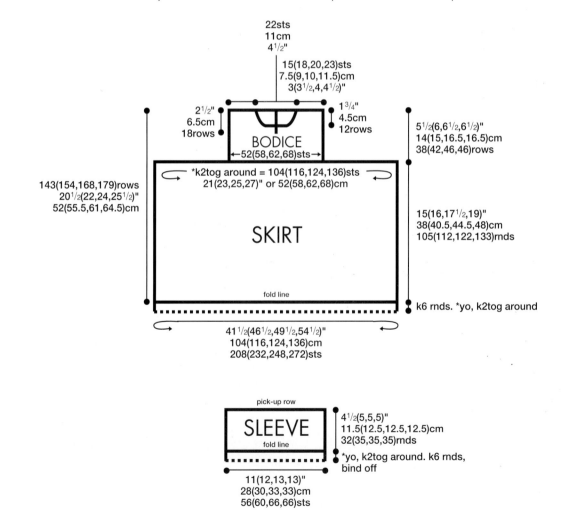

22sts
11cm
4½"

15(18,20,23)sts
7.5(9,10,11.5)cm
3(3½,4,4½)"

2½"
6.5cm
18rows

1¾"
4.5cm
12rows

BODICE
←52(58,62,68)sts→

5½(6,6½,6½)"
14(15,16.5,16.5)cm
38(42,46,46)rows

*k2tog around = 104(116,124,136)sts
21(23,25,27)" or 52(58,62,68)cm

143(154,168,179)rows
20½(22,24,25½)"
52(55.5,61,64.5)cm

SKIRT

15(16,17½,19)"
38(40.5,44.5,48)cm
105(112,122,133)rnds

fold line

k6 rnds. *yo, k2tog around

41½(46½,49½,54½)"
104(116,124,136)cm
208(232,248,272)sts

pick-up row

SLEEVE
fold line

4½(5,5,5)"
11.5(12.5,12.5,12.5)cm
32(35,35,35)rnds

*yo, k2tog around. k6 rnds,
bind off

11(12,13,13)"
28(30,33,33)cm
56(60,66,66)sts

Brittany Jumper

This double knitting cotton sleeveless jumper with lace hem and shoulder buttons is without doubt one of the most charming dresses I have ever done. Cute either with or without a blouse, this jumper works as a sundress or can be dressy enough for a party. If you have trouble with the lace hem, making a little chart on graph paper will help. The rest of the garment is a breeze after you have completed the hem.

■ Sizes

3 Months (6 Months, 1, 2, 3, 4 Years)

Finished chest: 14 (15, 17, 19, 22, 23) in./35.5 (38, 43, 48, 56, 58.5) cm

Length, shoulder to hem: 11.5 (12.5, 14.5, 15.5, 17, 19) in./29 (31.5, 37, 39.5, 43, 48) cm

■ Materials

DK weight cotton *that will obtain gauge below*

322 (376, 494, 590, 748, 874) yd/295 (344, 452, 540, 684, 799) m Light Green

Needles size 6 US (8 UK, 4 mm), *or size needed to obtain gauge*

Circular needle size 6 US (8 UK, 4 mm), 16 in. or 24 in./40 cm or 60 cm long

Crochet hook size F US (8 UK, 4 mm)

Four .5 in./1.5 cm buttons, a stitch holder, and stitch markers

Sample in photograph knit in Rowan DK Cotton #230 Boston Fern.

■ Gauge

20 sts and 28 rows = 4 in./10 cm in St st using size 6 needles

Always check gauge to save time and ensure correct yardage and correct fit! Always measure your child!

■ Picot Stitch (multiple of 8 sts, worked on circular needle):

Rnd 1: *K1, yo, k2, sl next 2 sts tog as if to k2tog, k1, pass the slipped sts over the k st (SK2P), k2, yo; rep from * around.

Rnd 2 and every other rnd: Knit.

Rnd 3: Rep rnd 1.

Rnd 5: *K2, yo, k1, SK2P, k1, yo, k1; rep from * around.

Rnd 7: *K3, yo, SK2P, yo, k2; rep from * around.

Rnd 8: Knit.

■ Body

With longer circular needle, cast on 176 (192, 208, 240, 264, 288) sts. Join and place marker for beg of rnd. Work 8 rnds of picot st, then rep rnds 7 and 8 only 2 (3, 4, 5, 6, 6) times. Cont in St st until piece measures 5.5 (6, 6.5, 7.25, 8.5, 9.5) in./14 (15, 16, 18.5, 21, 24) cm above picot hem.

Next rnd: K2tog around, to 88 (96, 104, 120, 132, 144) sts. Change to 16 in./40 cm circular needle if necessary.

■ Bodice

Work in k1, p1 rib for 2 rnds.

Divide for front and back: With straight needles, work 44 (48, 52, 60, 66, 72) sts for front, place rem sts on a holder for back.

Armhole shaping: Cont to work back and forth in rib, binding off 2 sts at beg of next 2 rows, dec 1 st each side every other row 3 (3, 3, 4, 4, 5) times, to 34 (38, 42, 48, 54, 58) sts. Work even until bodice measures 1.5 (1.75, 2.5, 2.5, 2.5, 3.5) in./4 (4.5, 5.5, 6.5, 6.5, 9) cm, end with a WS row.

Neck shaping: Work 12 (14, 16, 18, 21, 23) sts, join a 2nd skein of yarn and bind off center 10 (10, 10, 12, 12, 12) sts for neck,

work to end. Working both sides at same time, dec 1 st at each neck edge every other row 3 (4, 5, 5, 5, 6) times. Work even on rem 9 (10, 11, 13, 16, 17) sts each side until bodice measures 4 (4.5, 5.5, 5.5, 5.5, 6.5) in./10 (11.5, 14, 14, 14, 16.5) cm. *Next (buttonhole) row:* Rib 2 (2, 2, 3, 3, 3), yo, k2tog, rib 1 (2, 3, 3, 6, 7), yo, k2tog, rib to end. Rib 3 rows more. Bind off sts each side in rib.

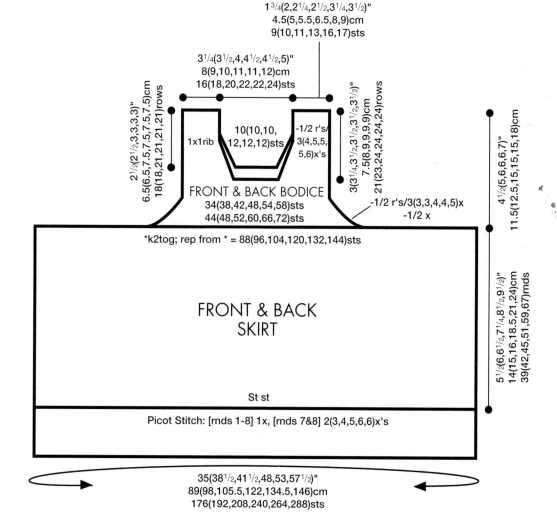

1 3/4(2,2 1/4,2 1/2,3 1/4,3 1/2)"
4.5(5,5.5,6.5,8,9)cm
9(10,11,13,16,17)sts

3 1/4(3 1/2,4,4 1/2,4 1/2,5)"
8(9,10,11,11,12)cm
16(18,20,22,22,24)sts

2 1/2(2 1/2,3,3,3,3)"
6.5(6.5,7.5,7.5,7.5,7.5)cm
18(18,21,21,21,21)rows

1x1rib

10(10,10,12,12,12)sts

-1/2 r's/3(4,5,5,5,6)x's

3(3 1/4,3 1/2,3 1/2,3 1/2,3 1/2)"
7.5(8,9,9,9,9)cm
21(23,24,24,24,24)rows

4 1/2(5,6,6,6,7)"
11.5(12.5,15,15,15,18)cm

FRONT & BACK BODICE
34(38,42,48,54,58)sts
44(48,52,60,66,72)sts

-1/2 r's/3(3,3,4,4,5)x
-1/2 x

*k2tog; rep from * = 88(96,104,120,132,144)sts

FRONT & BACK
SKIRT

5 1/2(6,6 1/2,7 1/4,8 1/2,9 1/2)"
14(15,16,18.5,21,24)cm
39(42,45,51,59,67)rnds

St st

Picot Stitch: [rnds 1-8] 1x, [rnds 7&8] 2(3,4,5,6,6)x's

35(38 1/2,41 1/2,48,53,57 1/2)"
89(98,105.5,122,134.5,146)cm
176(192,208,240,264,288)sts

■ Back

Work as for front, but work neck shaping when bodice measures 2 (2.25, 3, 3, 3, 4) in./5 (5.5, 7.5, 7.5, 7.5, 10) cm, as foll:

Neck shaping: Work 12 (14, 16, 18, 21, 23) sts, join a 2nd skein of yarn and bind off center 10 (10, 10, 12, 12, 12) sts for neck, work to end. Working both sides at same time, dec 1 st at each neck edge every other row 3 (4, 5, 5, 5, 6) times. Work even on rem 9 (10, 11, 13, 16, 17) sts each side until same length as front, but omitting buttonholes. Bind off sts each side in rib.

■ Finishing

With RS facing and crochet hook, work picot edging evenly around neck as foll: *Work sc in next 3 sts or rows, work 3 sc in next st or row; rep from * around. Join and fasten off. Work picot edging around each armhole edge in same way. Sew buttons on back shoulders, opposite buttonholes.

Tyrolean Waistcoat

This worsted weight wool double-knit vest with a buttoned front is great for boys and girls alike. This double-knitting is an old maritime technique and works up quickly if you hold one strand in your left hand and knit in the Continental method while holding the other in your right and working an English stitch. However you do it, *always* keep one yarn over the other, or the checkered effect will not work!

■ Sizes
3–6 Months (1, 2, 4, 6 Years)

Finished chest (buttoned): 19 (21.5, 23.5, 26.75, 30.5) in./48 (54.5, 59.5, 68, 77.5) cm

Length, shoulder to hem: 9.5 (10, 11, 13, 15) in./24 (25.5, 28, 33, 38) cm

■ Materials
Worsted weight wool *that will obtain gauge below*

90 (105, 130, 180, 230) yd/82 (96, 119, 165, 210) m each Black (MC) and Red (CC)

Needles size 9 US (5 UK, 5.5 mm), *or size needed to obtain gauge*

Crochet hook size J (4 UK, 6 mm)

Five (5, 5, 6, 6) .5 in./1.5 cm buttons, stitch holders, and stitch markers

■ Gauge
19 sts and 20 rows = 4 in./10 cm in pattern st using size 9 needles

Always check gauge to save time and ensure correct yardage and correct fit! Always measure your child!

■ Pattern Stitch (over an odd number of sts)
Row 1 (RS): K1 MC, *k1 CC, k1 MC; rep from * to end.

Row 2: K1 MC (selvage st), *p1 MC, p1 CC; rep from *, end p1 MC, k1 MC (selvage st)

Rep rows 1 and 2 for pat st.

Sample in photograph knit in Rowan Magpie Aran #62 Raven (MC) and #306 Peony (CC).

■ Back

With MC, cast on 43 (49, 55, 63, 71) sts and p 1 row on WS. Work in pat st until piece measures 5 (5, 5.5, 7, 8.5) in./12.5 (12.5, 14, 18, 21.5) cm from the beg. **Armhole shaping:** Bind off 2 sts at beg of next 2 rows. Dec 1 st each side every other row 3 times, to 33 (39, 45, 53, 61) sts. Work even until armhole measures 4.5 (5, 5.5, 6, 6.5) in./11.5 (12.5, 14, 15, 16.5) cm. Work 8 (10, 12, 15, 18) sts, then place on a holder for later finishing; with MC, bind off center 17 (19, 21, 23, 25) sts, place rem 8 (10, 12, 15, 18) sts on a holder.

■ Right front

With MC, cast on 5 (7, 7, 9, 9) sts. P 1 row on WS. Cont in pat st, AT THE SAME TIME, cast on 3 (3, 3, 4, 4) sts at beg of next 6 (6, 8, 2, 6) rows, 2 (2, 0, 3, 3) sts at beg of next 2 (2, 0, 6, 2) rows, to 27 (29, 31, 35, 39) sts. Place a marker at each end of row for measuring. Cont in pat st until piece measures 5 (5, 5.5, 7, 8.5) in./12.5 (12.5, 14, 18, 21.5) cm above marker. Work armhole shaping at side edge as for back, to 22 (24, 26, 30, 34) sts. Work even until armhole measures 2.5 (3, 3.5, 4, 4.5) in./6.5 (7.5, 9, 10, 11.5) cm, end with a WS row.

Neck shaping: Bind off 6 (6, 6, 7, 8) sts at beg of next row (neck edge) and cont to bind off from neck edge 3 sts twice, 2 sts once. When same length as back, place rem 8 (10, 12, 15, 18) sts on a holder. Place markers on front edge for 5 (5, 5, 6, 6) buttons, the first one just above lower edge curve, the last one .5 in./1.5 cm below neck, and the others spaced evenly between.

■ Left front

Work as for right front, reversing shaping, AT THE SAME TIME, place buttonholes opposite markers as foll: *In next row,* on RS, work to last 4 sts, yo, k2tog, work to end.

Shoulder seams: *With wrong sides facing,* place sts of back and front right shoulders on 2 parallel needles. With a 3rd needle, k through 1st st on each needle, then through the 2nd st on each needle, and pass 1st over 2nd to bind off. Cont in this way to end for knitted shoulder seam. Work in same way for left shoulder seam.

■ Finishing

Sew side seams. Weave in all loose ends. With crochet hook and MC, work 1 row single crochet and 1 row slip st around entire outside edge of vest and around armholes. Sew buttons in place.

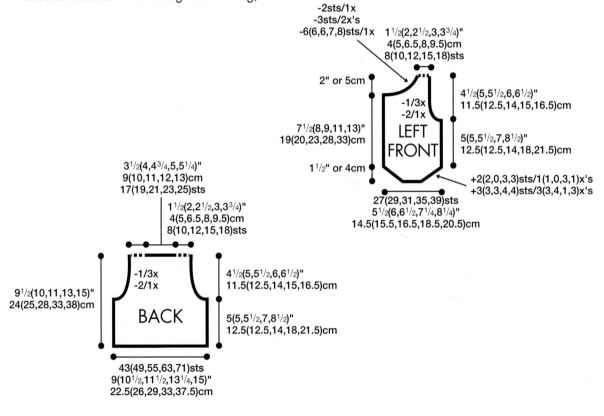

-2sts/1x
-3sts/2x's
-6(6,6,7,8)sts/1x

1¹/₂(2,2¹/₂,3,3³/₄)"
4(5,6.5,8,9.5)cm
8(10,12,15,18)sts

2" or 5cm

-1/3x
-2/1x

4¹/₂(5,5¹/₂,6,6¹/₂)"
11.5(12.5,14,15,16.5)cm

7¹/₂(8,9,11,13)"
19(20,23,28,33)cm

LEFT FRONT

5(5,5¹/₂,7,8¹/₂)"
12.5(12.5,14,18,21.5)cm

1¹/₂" or 4cm

+2(2,0,3,3)sts/1(1,0,3,1)x's
+3(3,3,4,4)sts/3(3,4,1,3)x's

27(29,31,35,39)sts
5¹/₂(6,6¹/₂,7¹/₄,8¹/₄)"
14.5(15.5,16.5,18.5,20.5)cm

3¹/₂(4,4³/₄,5,5¹/₄)"
9(10,11,12,13)cm
17(19,21,23,25)sts

1¹/₂(2,2¹/₂,3,3³/₄)"
4(5,6.5,8,9.5)cm
8(10,12,15,18)sts

-1/3x
-2/1x

4¹/₂(5,5¹/₂,6,6¹/₂)"
11.5(12.5,14,15,16.5)cm

BACK

9¹/₂(10,11,13,15)"
24(25,28,33,38)cm

5(5,5¹/₂,7,8¹/₂)"
12.5(12.5,14,18,21.5)cm

43(49,55,63,71)sts
9(10¹/₂,11¹/₂,13¹/₄,15)"
22.5(26,29,33,37.5)cm

Sweet Pea

A sleeveless confection with big back buttons and a ribbon belt, inspired from little Italian knitted dresses, this dress is done in two-toned wide-stripe color-blocked DK cotton, and is a Quick-Knit™. Sweet Pea makes an adorable companion for the Spring Coat on page 41. You can change the overall effect by changing the ribbon color.

■ Sizes
1 (2, 4, 6) Years

Finished chest (buttoned): 24 (26, 28, 30) in./60 (65, 70, 75) cm

Length, shoulder to hem: 16 (17.5, 20, 22) in./40 (44.5, 50.5, 55.5) cm

■ Materials
DK weight cotton *that will obtain gauge below*

235 (285, 350, 420) yd/215 (260, 320, 380) m each Medium Blue (MC) and Light Blue (CC)

Straight needles and double-pointed needles (dpn) size 6 US (8 UK, 4 mm), *or size needed to obtain gauge*

Circular needle size 6 US (8 UK, 4 mm), 24 in. or 29 in./60 cm or 74 cm long

Crochet hook size F (8 UK, 4 mm)

Sample (from back) in photograph knit in Rowan DK Cotton #287 Diana (MC) and #217 Powder (CC).

Three .75 in./2 cm buttons, 1 yd/1 m of 1 in./2.5 cm–wide satin ribbon, and stitch holders

■ Gauge
20 sts and 28 rows = 4 in./10 cm in St st using size 6 needles

Always check gauge to save time and ensure correct yardage and correct fit! Always measure your child!

■ Skirt

With circular needle and MC, cast on 240 (260, 280, 300) sts. Join and place marker for beg of rnd. [K 1 rnd, p 1 rnd] 3 times for garter st. Cont in St st (k every rnd) until piece measures 4 (4.5, 5, 5.5) in./10 (11.5, 13, 13.5) cm from beg. Cut MC, join CC and cont in St st until piece measures 10 (11, 12.5, 14) in./25 (28, 31.5, 35) cm from beg. *Next rnd:* K2tog around, to 120 (130, 140, 150) sts.

Divide for front and back: *Next rnd:* Cut CC, join MC and k60 (65, 70, 75) and place on a holder for back, k to end for front. Cont on straight needles.

■ Front bodice

Work front sts back and forth in St st (k 1 row, p 1 row) for 1 (1, 1.5, 1.5) in./2.5 (2.5, 4, 4) cm, ending with a WS row.

Armhole shaping: Bind off 2 sts at beg of next 0 (0, 2, 2) rows, dec 1 st each side on next row, then every other row 3 (4, 3, 4) times more, to 52 (55, 58, 61) sts. Work even until bodice measures 3.5 (4, 5, 5.5) in./8.5 (10, 12.5, 14) cm.

Neck shaping: Work 21 (22, 23, 24) sts, join a 2nd skein of yarn and bind off center 10 (11, 12, 13) sts, work to end. Working both sides at the same time, bind off from each neck edge 2 sts twice, 1 st 3 times. Work even on rem 14 (15, 16, 17) sts each side until bodice measures 6 (6.5, 7.5, 8) in./15 (16.5, 19, 20.5) cm. Place sts on a holder for later finishing.

■ Back bodice

Work as for front until bodice measures 2.5 (3, 4, 4.5) in./6 (7.5, 10, 11.5) cm.

Placket shaping: Work 24 (25, 27, 28) sts, bind off 4 (5, 4, 5) sts, work to end. Work both sides at same time until bodice measures 5 (5.5, 6.5, 7) in./12.5 (14, 16.5, 18) cm.

Neck shaping: Bind off from each neck edge 4 sts 1 (1, 2, 2) time, 3 sts 2 (2, 1, 1) times. Place rem 14 (15, 16, 17) sts each side on holders for later finishing.

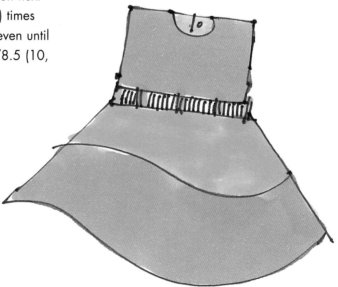

■ Finishing

Sew side seams of bodice.

Shoulder seams: *With wrong sides facing each other,* place sts of back and front right shoulders on 2 parallel dpn. With a 3rd dpn and MC, k through 1st st on each needle, then through the 2nd st on each needle, and pass 1st over 2nd to bind off. Cont in this way to end for a knitted seam. Work in same way for left shoulder seam.

Placket edging: With RS facing, straight needles, and MC, pick up and k 25 sts evenly along left back placket. Work in k1, p1 rib for 1 in./2.5 cm. Bind off in rib. Work in same way along right back placket, but work 3 buttonholes after .5 in./1.5 cm as foll: Rib 3, [bind off 2 sts, rib 6] twice, bind off 2 sts, rib to end. On next row, cast on 2 sts over bound-off sts. When band measures 1 in./2.5 cm, bind off in rib.

Neckband: With RS facing and crochet hook, work 1 row sc evenly around neck edge.

Armhole bands: Work same as neckband. Sew buttons on left back opposite buttonholes.

Belt loops (make 7): With crochet hook and MC, ch 1.5 in./4 cm. Fasten off. Sew belt loops evenly around front and back bodice. Weave ribbon through loops and tie at back.

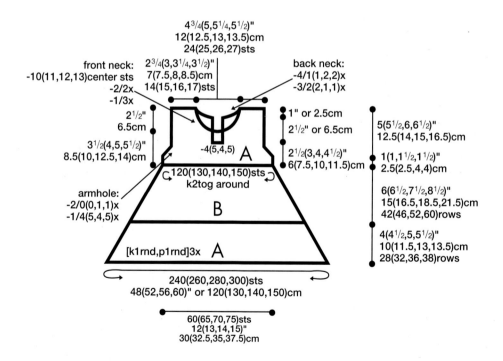

Lemonade
15¢

Summer

■ Summer is the time for spur-of-the-moment jaunts and family gatherings, and summer knitting projects can be relaxing, with delightful results. The beach beckons, and lovely cotton handknits are cool yet zesty for picnics on windy days. Whether the kids are playing in the sand in a cardigan chenille robe or sporting crisp cotton sunsuits, whites and brights are the colors to choose for summer. These simple cotton pullovers are quickly knit in modern, bold designs, my favorite classics with a twist. Double knitting, or DK, cotton is perfect for summer, as it has enough body to retain shape yet is light enough for the season. I know how quickly your summer days can fill up, but you'll still have time to adorn your little ones in a batch of these summery QuickKnits™.

Zigzag

A chic, bright, bold cotton classic crewneck with an enormous and absolutely unclassic zigzag intarsia pattern, this sweater is fun to knit and zany to wear. Bobbins make knitting it up a snap. This one is great for the bigger kids in your life.

■ Sizes

2 (4, 6, 8) Years

Finished chest: 27 (30, 32, 34) in./68 (76, 80, 86) cm

Length, shoulder to hem: 13 (15, 16, 18) in./33 (37.5, 40.5, 45.5) cm

■ Materials

DK weight cotton *that will obtain gauge below*

720 (940, 1080, 1270) yd/650 (850, 980, 1150) m White (MC)

370 (490, 560, 660) yd/339 (448, 512, 604) m Red (CC)

Needles sizes 4, 6 US (10, 8 UK; 3.5, 4 mm), *or size needed to obtain gauge*

Double-pointed needles (dpn) size 6 US (8 UK, 4 mm)

Stitch holders and stitch markers

Sample in photographs knit in Rowan DK Cotton #263 Pimpernel (CC) and #249 Bleached White (MC).

■ Gauge

20 sts and 28 rows = 4 in./10 cm in St st and chart pat using larger needles

Always check gauge to save time and ensure correct yardage and correct fit! Always measure your child!

■ Back

With smaller straight needles and MC, cast on 68 (76, 80, 86) sts. Work in k1, p1 rib for 1.5 in./4 cm. Change to larger needles. Work in St st and chart pat as foll: **Beg chart pat 2 years only:** Beg with 4th st of chart, work to end of chart, then work 23-st rep twice, k2 MC. **Beg chart pat 4, 6, 8 years:** Work (1, 3, 6) MC, work 23-st rep 3 times, work (6, 8, 11) MC. Cont in pat until piece measures 13 (15, 16, 18) in./33 (37.5, 40.5, 45.5) cm from beg. Place 21 (24, 25, 28) sts on a holder for one shoulder, place next 26 (28, 30, 30) sts on a 2nd holder for back neck, place rem 21 (24, 25, 28) sts on a 3rd holder for other shoulder.

■ Front

Work as for back until piece measures 11 (12.5, 13.5, 15.5) in./28 (31, 34, 39) cm from beg.

Neck shaping: Next RS row, work 29 (32, 33, 36) sts, bind off center 10 (12, 14, 14) sts, work to end. Working both sides at same time, bind off from each neck edge 3 sts once, 2 sts once, 1 st 3 times. Work even until same length as back. Place rem 21 (24, 25, 28) sts each side on holders for later finishing.

Shoulder seams: *With wrong sides facing each other,* place sts of back and front right shoulders on 2 parallel dpn. With a 3rd dpn and MC, k through 1st st on each needle, then through the 2nd st on each needle, and pass 1st over 2nd to bind off. Cont in this way to end for a knitted seam. Work in same way for left shoulder seam.

■ Sleeves

Place markers on front and back 6.5 (7, 7.5, 8) in./16.5 (17.5, 19, 20) cm down from shoulder seam for armholes. With RS facing, larger straight needles, and MC, pick up and k 66 (70, 76, 80) sts between markers. Work in St st and chart pat as foll: **Beg chart pat 2, 4 years:** Beg with 5th (3rd) st of chart, work to end of chart, then work 23-st rep twice, k1

(3) MC. **Beg chart pat 6, 8 years:** Work (1, 3) MC, work 23-st rep 3 times, work (6, 8) MC. Cont in pat as es, dec 1 st each end every 4th row 10 (17, 19, 20) times, every other row 7 (0, 0, 0) times, to 32 (36, 38, 40) sts. Work even until sleeve measures 8 (10, 11, 12) in./20 (25.5, 27.5, 30) cm. Change to smaller needles and work 1 (1.5, 1.5, 1.5) in./2.5 (4, 4, 4) cm in k1, p1 rib with MC. Bind off loosely and evenly in rib.

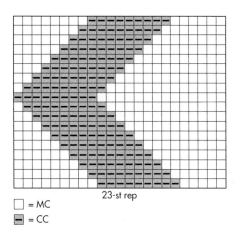

23-st rep

☐ = MC

▨ = CC

■ Finishing

For neckband, with RS facing, dpn, and MC, pick up and k 70 (74, 78, 78) sts evenly around neck edge, including sts from holders. Join and work in k1, p1 rib for 1 in./2.5 cm. Bind off loosely and evenly in rib. Sew side and sleeve seams.

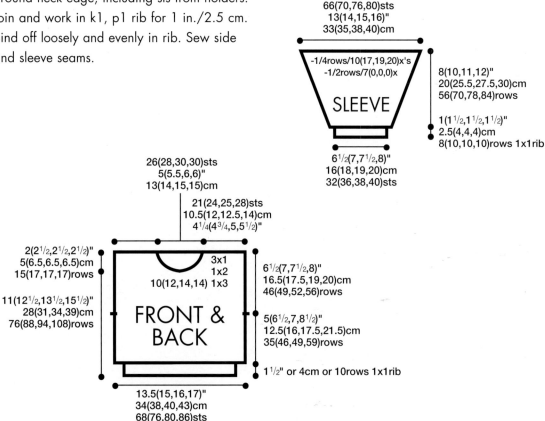

66(70,76,80)sts
13(14,15,16)"
33(35,38,40)cm

-1/4rows/10(17,19,20)x's
-1/2rows/7(0,0,0)x

SLEEVE

8(10,11,12)"
20(25.5,27.5,30)cm
56(70,78,84)rows

1(1$^1/_2$,1$^1/_2$,1$^1/_2$)"
2.5(4,4,4)cm
8(10,10,10)rows 1x1rib

6$^1/_2$(7,7$^1/_2$,8)"
16(18,19,20)cm
32(36,38,40)sts

26(28,30,30)sts
5(5.5,6,6)"
13(14,15,15)cm

21(24,25,28)sts
10.5(12,12.5,14)cm
4$^1/_4$(4$^3/_4$,5,5$^1/_2$)"

2(2$^1/_2$,2$^1/_2$,2$^1/_2$)"
5(6.5,6.5,6.5)cm
15(17,17,17)rows

3x1
1x2
10(12,14,14) 1x3

6$^1/_2$(7,7$^1/_2$,8)"
16.5(17.5,19,20)cm
46(49,52,56)rows

11(12$^1/_2$,13$^1/_2$,15$^1/_2$)"
28(31,34,39)cm
76(88,94,108)rows

FRONT &
BACK

5(6$^1/_2$,7,8$^1/_2$)"
12.5(16,17.5,21.5)cm
35(46,49,59)rows

1$^1/_2$" or 4cm or 10rows 1x1rib

13.5(15,16,17)"
34(38,40,43)cm
68(76,80,86)sts

Swedish Day Dress

One-row stripes give this cotton dress with front buttons and short sleeves a Scandinavian flair. The swingy, comfortable silhouette makes this the perfect playdress.

■ Sizes

1 (2, 4, 6) Years

Finished chest (buttoned): 21 (23, 25, 27) in./53.5 (57.5, 63.5, 67.5) cm

Length, shoulder to hem: 17.5 (19, 20.5, 21.5) in./44 (48, 52, 54.5) cm

■ Materials

DK weight cotton *that will obtain gauge below*

240 (380, 455, 505) yd/220 (345, 410, 455) m each Fuchsia (A) and Lime Green (B)

Straight needles and double-pointed needles (dpn) size 6 US (8 UK, 4 mm), *or size needed to obtain gauge*

Circular needle size 6 US (8 UK, 4 mm),16 in. or 24 in./40 cm or 60 cm long

Six .75 in./2 cm buttons, 1 small snap, stitch holders, and stitch markers

■ Gauge

20 sts and 28 rows = 4 in./10 cm in St st using size 6 needles

Sample in photographs knit in Rowan DK Cotton #233 Cerise (A) and #230 Boston Fern (B).

Always check gauge to save time and ensure correct yardage and correct fit! Always measure your child!

■ Stripe Pattern

*1 row A, 1 row B; rep from * for stripe pat.
Note: To avoid joining a new color at the beg of each stripe, beg each row at the side of knitting where the yarn for the next color is. Remember to always k on the RS and p on the WS of the fabric.

■ Skirt

With circular needle and A, cast on 215 (231, 255, 271) sts. Work back and forth as with straight needles as foll: *Row 1 (RS):* With B, *k1, p1; rep from *, end k1. *Row 2:* With A, *p1, k1; rep from *, end p1. Rep rows 1 and 2 until piece measures 1 in./2.5 cm from beg. Keeping first and last 8 sts in rib pat as established, work rem sts in St st and cont stripe pat, dec 1 st in center of 1st row, to 214 (230, 254, 270) sts. On 2nd row above rib, work a buttonhole in center of right front rib by yo, k2tog. Work 5 more buttonholes spaced 2.75 (3, 3.25, 3.5) in./7 (7.5, 8, 9) cm apart. Work even until piece measures 12.5 (13.5, 14.5, 15) in./31.5 (34, 37, 38) cm from beg, end with a WS row. *Next row (RS):* Work 8 rib sts, k2tog to last 8 sts, work 8 rib sts, to 115 (123, 135, 143) sts.

Divide for front and back: *Next row (WS):* Work 31 (33, 36, 38) sts and place on a holder for left front, work next 53 (57, 63, 67) sts for back, place rem 31 (33, 36, 38) sts on a holder for right front. If desired, work rem pieces with straight needles.

■ Back bodice

Cont on back sts only until bodice measures 5 (5.5, 6, 6.5) in./12.5 (14, 15, 16.5) cm. Work 15 (16, 19, 20) sts and place on a holder, bind off 23 (25, 25, 27) sts for neck, work last 15 (16, 19, 20) sts and place on a holder for later finishing.

■ Left front bodice

Work left front sts until bodice measures 3 (3.5, 4, 4.5) in./7.5 (9, 10, 11.5) cm, end with a RS row. *Note:* When working neck shaping, you must join new color at neck edge when necessary instead of going to the other end of the needle.

Neck shaping: Bind off 8 (9, 9, 10) sts at beg of next (WS) row (neck edge), work to end. Cont to bind off from neck edge 3 sts once, 2 sts twice, 1 st once. When same length as back, place rem 15 (16, 19, 20) sts on a holder for later finishing.

■ Right front bodice

Work as for left front, cont buttonholes, and reverse neck shaping.

Shoulder seams: *With wrong sides facing each other,* place sts of back and front right shoulders on 2 parallel dpn. With a 3rd dpn and A, k through 1st st on each needle, then through the 2nd st on each needle, and pass 1st over 2nd to bind off. Cont in this way to end for a knitted seam. Work in same way for left shoulder seam.

■ Sleeves

Place markers on front and back 5 (5.5, 6, 6.5) in./12.5 (14, 15, 16.5) cm down from shoulder seams for armholes. With RS facing and straight needles, pick up and k 50 (56,

60, 66) sts between markers. Work in St st and stripe pat for 3.5 (3.5, 4, 4) in./9 (9, 10, 10) cm. Work in k1, p1 rib and cont stripe pat for 1 in./2.5 cm, end with an A stripe. Bind off in rib with A.

■ Finishing

For neckband, with RS facing, circular needle, and A, pick up and k 1 st in each st and row around neck edge. Bind off from RS knitwise. Sew buttons on left front opposite buttonholes. Sew snap inside button placket at neck.

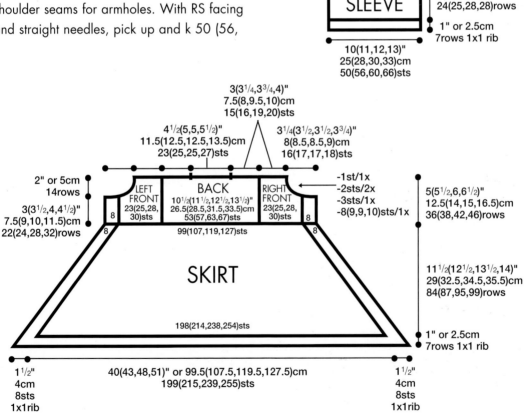

SLEEVE

pick-up row

3½(3½,4,4)"
9(9,10,10)cm
24(25,28,28)rows

1" or 2.5cm
7rows 1x1 rib

10(11,12,13)"
25(28,30,33)cm
50(56,60,66)sts

3(3¼,3¾,4)"
7.5(8,9.5,10)cm
15(16,19,20)sts

4½(5,5,5½)"
11.5(12.5,12.5,13.5)cm
23(25,25,27)sts

3¼(3½,3½,3¾)"
8(8.5,8.5,9)cm
16(17,17,18)sts

2" or 5cm
14rows

3(3¼,4,4½)"
7.5(9,10,11.5)cm
22(24,28,32)rows

LEFT FRONT
23(25,28,30)sts

BACK
10½(11½,12½,13½)"
26.5(28.5,31.5,33.5)cm
53(57,63,67)sts

RIGHT FRONT
23(25,28,30)sts

8   8   99(107,119,127)sts   8

-1st/1x
-2sts/2x
-3sts/1x
-8(9,9,10)sts/1x

5(5½,6,6½)"
12.5(14,15,16.5)cm
36(38,42,46)rows

SKIRT

198(214,238,254)sts

11½(12½,13½,14)"
29(32.5,34.5,35.5)cm
84(87,95,99)rows

1" or 2.5cm
7rows 1x1 rib

1½"
4cm
8sts
1x1rib

40(43,48,51)" or 99.5(107.5,119.5,127.5)cm
199(215,239,255)sts

1½"
4cm
8sts
1x1rib

Beach Robe

Bulky cotton chenille knits up in a twinkling and is soft and warm for this Quick-Knit™ hooded sweater, with a big button closure and roll-back sleeves, all in garter stitch. This is a great learn-to-knit or return-to-knitting project. And the robe can be lengthened to make a cozy bathrobe.

■ Sizes

1 (2, 4, 6) Years

Finished chest (buttoned): 24.5 (26, 28, 30) in./62 (66, 70, 75) cm

Length, shoulder to hem: 11.5 (13, 14, 15) in./29 (33, 35, 38) cm

■ Materials

Bulky chenille *that will obtain gauge below*

390 (465, 550, 635) yd/350 (420, 495, 575) m Navy

Straight needles and double-pointed needles (dpn) size 6 US (8 UK, 4 mm), *or size needed to obtain gauge*

One 1 in./2.5 cm button, stitch holders, and stitch markers

One tapestry needle

■ Gauge

17 sts and 28 rows = 4 in./10 cm in garter st using size 6 needles

Always check gauge to save time and ensure correct yardage and correct fit! Always measure your child!

Sample in photograph knit in Rowan Chunky Chenille #378 Serge.

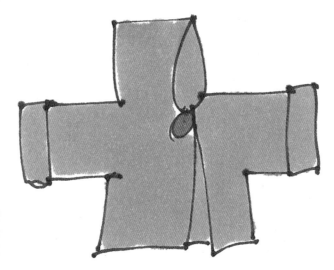

■ Back

With straight needles, cast on 52 (56, 60, 64) sts and work in garter st until piece measures 10.75 (12.25, 13.25, 14.25) in./26.5 (31, 33, 36) cm from beg.

Neck shaping: *Next row (RS):* Work 18 (19, 21, 22) sts, join a 2nd skein of yarn and bind off center 16 (18, 18, 20) sts, work to end. Working both sides at the same time, bind off 2 sts from each neck edge twice. Work even until piece measures 11.5 (13, 14, 15) in./28.5 (33, 35, 38) cm from beg. Place rem 14 (15, 17, 18) sts each side on holders for later finishing.

■ Left front

With straight needles, cast on 30 (32, 34, 36) sts and work in garter st until piece measures 9.5 (10.5, 11.5, 12.5) in./23.5 (26.5, 28.5, 31.5) cm from beg, end with a RS row.

Neck shaping: *Next row (WS):* Bind off 8 sts (neck edge), work to end. Cont to bind off from neck edge 3 sts once, 2 sts once, 1 st 3 (4, 4, 5) times. Work even until same length as back. Place rem 14 (15, 17, 18) sts on a holder for later finishing.

■ Right front

Work as for left front, reversing neck shaping.
Shoulder seams: *With wrong sides facing,* place sts of back and front right shoulders on 2 parallel dpn. With a 3rd dpn, k through 1st st on each needle, then through the 2nd st on each needle, and pass 1st over 2nd to bind off. Cont in this way to end for a knitted seam. Work in same way for left shoulder seam.

■ Sleeves

Place markers on front and back 6 (6.5, 6.5, 7) in./15 (16.5, 16.5, 18) cm down from shoulder seam for armholes. With RS facing and straight needles, pick up and k 52 (56, 56, 60) sts between markers. Work in garter st until sleeve measures 7 (8, 10.5, 11.5) in./18 (20, 26.5, 28.5) cm. Bind off loosely.

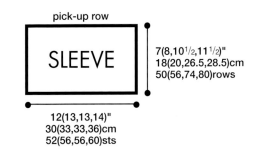

pick-up row

SLEEVE

7(8,10½,11½)"
18(20,26.5,28.5)cm
50(56,74,80)rows

12(13,13,14)"
30(33,33,36)cm
52(56,56,60)sts

■ Hood

Pick up and k 33 (36, 36, 38) sts around right front neck to center back neck (separate halves produce more fullness). Work in garter st for 7 (7, 7.5, 8) in./18 (18, 19, 20.5) cm.

Shape top: *Next row (WS):* Bind off 3 sts (center edge), work to end. Cont to bind off 3 sts from center edge twice more, then 2 sts 5 (6, 6, 7) times. Bind off rem 14 (15, 15, 15) sts. Beg at center back neck, pick up and k sts around to left neck and work other half hood to correspond, reversing shaping. Sew hood seam.

■ Finishing

Sew sleeve and side seams. Sew button on left front neck below hood. With a tapestry needle and a piece of yarn, make a button loop on right front, opposite button.

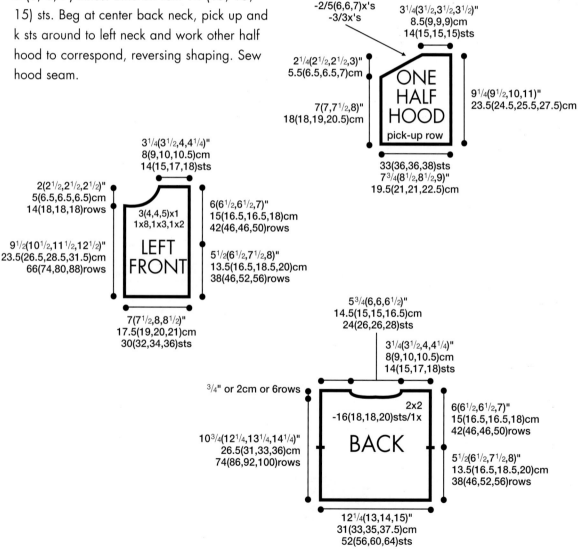

-2/5(6,6,7)x's
-3/3x's

$3^1/4(3^1/2,3^1/2,3^1/2)$"
8.5(9,9,9)cm
14(15,15,15)sts

$2^1/4(2^1/2,2^1/2,3)$"
5.5(6.5,6.5,7)cm

ONE HALF HOOD
pick-up row

$9^1/4(9^1/2,10,11)$"
23.5(24.5,25.5,27.5)cm

7(7,$7^1/2$,8)"
18(18,19,20.5)cm

33(36,36,38)sts
$7^3/4(8^1/2,8^1/2,9)$"
19.5(21,21,22.5)cm

$3^1/4(3^1/2,4,4^1/4)$"
8(9,10,10.5)cm
14(15,17,18)sts

2(${2^1/2},{2^1/2},{2^1/2}$)"
5(6.5,6.5,6.5)cm
14(18,18,18)rows

3(4,4,5)x1
1x8,1x3,1x2

LEFT FRONT

6($6^1/2$,$6^1/2$,7)"
15(16.5,16.5,18)cm
42(46,46,50)rows

$9^1/2(10^1/2,11^1/2,12^1/2)$"
23.5(26.5,28.5,31.5)cm
66(74,80,88)rows

$5^1/2(6^1/2,7^1/2,8)$"
13.5(16.5,18.5,20)cm
38(46,52,56)rows

7($7^1/2$,8,$8^1/2$)"
17.5(19,20,21)cm
30(32,34,36)sts

$5^3/4(6,6,6^1/2)$"
14.5(15,15,16.5)cm
24(26,26,28)sts

$3^1/4(3^1/2,4,4^1/4)$"
8(9,10,10.5)cm
14(15,17,18)sts

$3/4$" or 2cm or 6rows

2x2
-16(18,18,20)sts/1x

BACK

6($6^1/2$,$6^1/2$,7)"
15(16.5,16.5,18)cm
42(46,46,50)rows

$10^3/4(12^1/4,13^1/4,14^1/4)$"
26.5(31,33,36)cm
74(86,92,100)rows

$5^1/2(6^1/2,7^1/2,8)$"
13.5(16.5,18.5,20)cm
38(46,52,56)rows

$12^1/4(13,14,15)$"
31(33,35,37.5)cm
52(56,60,64)sts

Sunsuit

Your littlest angel will love this soft cotton QuickKnit™ playsuit. A classic, with a bib front and crossed straps in back, full shorts with side waist and strap buttons, this suit is perfect alone at the beach or paired with a shirt or blouse in town.

■ Sizes

6 Months (1, 2, 3 Years)

Finished waist: 19.5 (22, 23.25, 25.5) in./49 (55, 58, 64) cm

■ Materials

DK weight cotton *that will obtain gauge below*

660 (810, 890, 1050) yd/600 (730, 800, 960) m Orange

Needles sizes 3, 6 US (UK 10, 8; 3.25, 4 mm), *or size needed to obtain gauge*

Circular needle size 6 US (8 UK, 4 mm), 16 in. or 24 in./40 cm or 60 cm long

Four 1 in./2.5 cm buttons, two .75 in./2 cm buttons, stitch holders, and stitch markers

■ Gauge

20 sts and 28 rows = 4 in./10 cm in St st using larger needles

Always check gauge to save time and ensure correct yardage and correct fit! Always measure your child!

Sample in photographs knit in Rowan DK Cotton #254 Flame.

■ Pattern Stitch (multiple of 6 sts)

Rows 1–4: Work in St st.

Row 5 (RS): *K1, p1, k4; rep from *.

Rows 6–10: Work in St st.

Row 11: K4, p1, *k5, p1; rep from *, end k1.

Row 12: Work in St st.

Rep rows 1–12 for pat st.

■ Legs (make 2)

Cuff: With smaller needles, cast on 60 (66, 69, 75) sts. Work in garter st for 1.5 in./4 cm. Change to larger needles.

Leg: On RS, k and inc 1 st in every st across row. Work even on 120 (132, 138, 150) sts in pat st until piece measures 5 (5.5, 5.5, 6) in./12.5 (13.5, 13.5, 15) cm above cuff.

Crotch shaping: Beg RS, bind off 3 sts beg next 2 rows. Dec 1 st each end every other row 3 times, to 108 (120, 126, 138) sts. With RS facing, sl sts for one leg on circular needle, place marker for center back, and sl sts of other leg to same circular needle. Join and work even in pat st on 216 (240, 252, 276) sts until piece measures 12 (13.5, 14, 15) in./30 (33.5, 35, 37.5) cm above cuff. K2tog around, to 108 (120, 126, 138) sts.

■ Bodice

Divide for front and back: Sl first 27 (30, 31, 34) sts and last 27 (30, 32, 35) sts to straight needles, place rem 54 (60, 63, 69) sts on a holder for front. Cont on back sts as foll: Working back and forth, work in garter st for 1 in./2.5 cm. Bind off loosely.

■ Front

Sl 54 (60, 63, 69) sts from holder to larger straight needles. Work in garter st for .5 in./1.5 cm. *Next (buttonhole) row:* K3, bind off 2 sts, k to last 5 sts, bind off 2 sts, k to end. *Next row:* Cast on 2 sts over bound-off sts. Work even until garter st measures 1 in./2.5 cm, end with a WS row. Bind off 12 (13, 13, 14) sts at beg of next 2 rows, to 30 (34, 37, 41) sts. Cont as foll: *Next row (RS):* Work 5 sts in garter st, 20 (24, 27, 31) sts in pat st, 5 sts in garter st. Cont as est for 3 (3.5, 4, 4.5) in./7.5 (9, 10, 11.5) cm. Work in garter st on all sts for 1 in./2.5 cm. Bind off loosely.

■ Straps (make 2)

*With smaller needles, cast on 10 sts and work in garter st for 4 rows. Bind off 2 sts in center of next row for buttonhole. *Next row:* Cast on 2 sts over bound-off sts. Cont in garter st until strap measures 10 in./25.5 cm, or desired length. Work buttonhole as before. Work 4 rows even. Bind off. Rep from * for 2nd strap.

■ Finishing

Sew inside leg seams. Sew .75 in./2 cm buttons at top of front bodice. Sew 1 in./2.5 cm buttons on back waist opposite buttons on front bodice and opposite buttonholes. Sew buttons on straps.

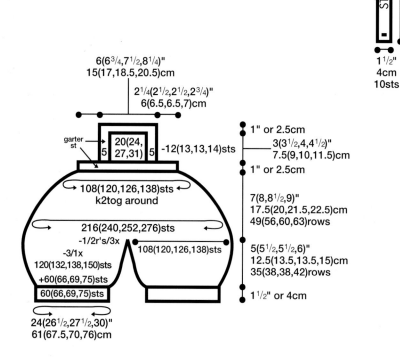

STRAP

10¹/₂" or 27cm

1¹/₂"
4cm
10sts

6(6³/₄,7¹/₂,8¹/₄)"
15(17,18.5,20.5)cm

2¹/₄(2¹/₂,2¹/₂,2³/₄)"
6(6.5,6.5,7)cm

garter st

20(24, 27,31)

5   5   -12(13,13,14)sts

1" or 2.5cm

3(3¹/₂,4,4¹/₂)"
7.5(9,10,11.5)cm

1" or 2.5cm

108(120,126,138)sts
k2tog around

7(8,8¹/₂,9)"
17.5(20,21.5,22.5)cm
49(56,60,63)rows

216(240,252,276)sts
-1/2r's/3x
-3/1x
120(132,138,150)sts
+60(66,69,75)sts

108(120,126,138)sts

5(5¹/₂,5¹/₂,6)"
12.5(13.5,13.5,15)cm
35(38,38,42)rows

60(66,69,75)sts

1¹/₂" or 4cm

24(26¹/₂,27¹/₂,30)"
61(67.5,70,76)cm

Au Bateau

A classic boat-necked pullover QuickKnit™ sweater is worked in warm, deep plum with narrow white stripes and full sleeves in an easy hip length with ribbed neck and bottom band. In cotton, this sweater is great in bright red, too . . . or try your own unusual color favorite.

■ Sizes

2 (4, 6, 8) Years

Finished chest: 27 (30, 32, 34) in./67 (75, 81, 85) cm

Length, shoulder to hem: 13 (15, 16, 17.5) in./32.5 (37, 40, 44.5) cm

■ Materials

DK weight cotton *that will obtain gauge below*

660 (865, 995, 1150) yd/595 (780, 895, 1035) m Navy (MC)

100 (130, 150, 175) yd/90 (120, 135, 160) m White (CC)

Needles sizes 5, 6 US (9, 8 UK; 3.75, 4 mm), *or size needed to obtain gauge*

Double-pointed needles (dpn) size 5 US (9 UK, 3.75 mm)

Stitch holders and stitch markers

Sample in photographs knit in Rowan DK Cotton #277 Plum (MC) and #253 White (CC).

■ Gauge

20 sts and 28 rows = 4 in./10 cm in St st using size 6 needles

Always check gauge to save time and ensure correct yardage and correct fit! Always measure your child!

■ Back

With smaller needles and MC, cast on 67 (75, 81, 85) sts. Work in k1, p1 rib for 1.5 (2, 2, 2) in./4 (5, 5, 5) cm. Change to larger needles. Work in St st and stripe pat as foll: 3 (3, 1, 3) rows MC, [2 rows CC, 8 rows MC] 7 (8, 9, 10) times. Change to smaller needles. Work in k1, p1 rib with MC for 1 in./2.5 cm. Piece should measure approx 13 (15, 16, 17.5) in./32.5 (37, 40, 44.5) cm from beg. Work 15 (19, 22, 24) sts and place on a holder for one shoulder, bind off next 37 sts in rib for back neck. Place rem 15 (19, 22, 24) sts on a 2nd holder for other shoulder.

■ Front

Work as for back.

Shoulder seams: *With wrong sides facing each other,* place sts of back and front right shoulders on 2 parallel dpn. With a 3rd dpn and MC, k through 1st st on each needle, then through the 2nd st on each needle, and pass 1st over 2nd to bind off. Cont in this way to end for a knitted seam. Work in same way for left shoulder seam.

■ Sleeves

Place markers on front and back 6 (6.5, 7, 7.5) in./15 (16, 17.5, 19) cm down from shoulder seam for armholes. With RS facing, larger needles, and MC, pick up and K 60 (66, 70, 76) sts between markers. Work in St st and stripe pat and dec as foll: Work [8 rows MC, 2 rows CC] 5 (7, 8, 8) times, 8 (4, 1, 8) rows MC, AT THE SAME TIME, work 6 rows even, then dec 1 st each end on next row, then every 4th row 12 (14, 16, 18) times more, to 34 (36, 36, 38) sts. After all

stripes have been worked, sleeve measures approx 8.25 (10.5, 11.5, 12.5) in./20.5 (26.5, 29, 31.5) cm. Change to smaller needles and work 1 in./2.5 cm in k1, p1 rib with MC. Bind off loosely and evenly in rib.

■ Finishing

Sew side and sleeve seams.

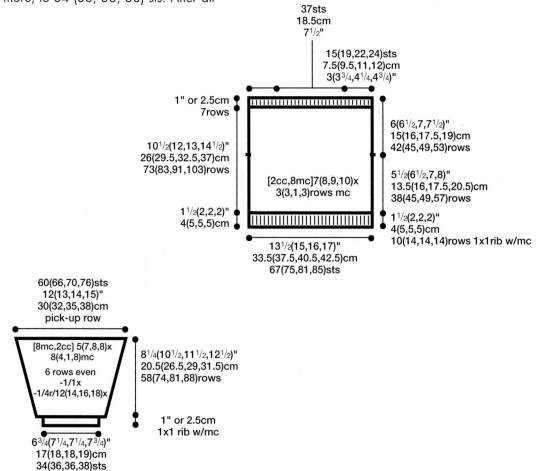

37sts
18.5cm
7 1/2"

15(19,22,24)sts
7.5(9.5,11,12)cm
3(3 3/4,4 1/4,4 3/4)"

1" or 2.5cm
7rows

6(6 1/2,7,7 1/2)"
15(16,17.5,19)cm
42(45,49,53)rows

10 1/2(12,13,14 1/2)"
26(29.5,32.5,37)cm
73(83,91,103)rows

[2cc,8mc]7(8,9,10)x
3(3,1,3)rows mc

5 1/2(6 1/2,7,8)"
13.5(16,17.5,20.5)cm
38(45,49,57)rows

1 1/2(2,2,2)"
4(5,5,5)cm

1 1/2(2,2,2)"
4(5,5,5)cm
10(14,14,14)rows 1x1 rib w/mc

13 1/2(15,16,17)"
33.5(37.5,40.5,42.5)cm
67(75,81,85)sts

60(66,70,76)sts
12(13,14,15)"
30(32,35,38)cm
pick-up row

[8mc,2cc] 5(7,8,8)x
8(4,1,8)mc

6 rows even
-1/1x
-1/4r/12(14,16,18)x

8 1/4(10 1/2,11 1/2,12 1/2)"
20.5(26.5,29,31.5)cm
58(74,81,88)rows

1" or 2.5cm
1x1 rib w/mc

6 3/4(7 1/4,7 1/4,7 3/4)"
17(18,18,19)cm
34(36,36,38)sts

Autumn

Fall comes overnight on a swift wind, and our knitting baskets overflow with a new agenda for short days and long evenings. We're anxious to pick up our needles again, and sweaters and hats quickly become a necessity. Wools are warm and rich, and these turtlenecks, shawl collars, and double-breasted jackets knit up in a snap for wrapping kids in clear colors for fall. Wool sweaters, generously sized, provide wonderful warmth and couldn't be more comfortable because the natural fibers breath and stretch. No one can have enough cozy hand-knits at this time of year, not even the family dog!

Bow Wow

Very easy, this QuickKnit™ full-cabled wool sweater with a turtleneck has a matching dog sweater for the pooch! This sweater is sized up, as it is perfect for toddlers as well as teens. Knit one up for all the kids and the family dog.

■ Sizes

6 Months (18 Months, 2, 4, 6, 8, 10 Years)

Child's sweater finished chest: 20.5 (22.5, 25, 28, 30, 33, 35) in./52 (57, 63.5, 71, 76, 84, 89) cm

Child's sweater length, shoulder to hem: 10 (11, 13, 16, 17.5, 19, 20.5) in./25.5 (28, 33, 40.5, 44.5, 48, 52) cm

Dog's sweater finished chest: 17.5 (19, 21) in./44.5 (48, 53) cm

Dog's sweater length, neck to base of tail: 6 (12, 19) in./15 (30.5, 48) cm

Note: Measure your dog to choose appropriate size. You may need to make further adjustments in length according to the size of your dog.

■ Materials

Worsted weight wool *that will obtain gauge below*

Sample in studio photograph knit in Cynthia Helene Merino Wool in #134 Gold; sample in location photograph (page 88) knit in Rowan Magpie Pesto #768.

Child's sweater: 375 (465, 595, 825, 985, 1175, 1365) yd/343 (425, 544, 754, 900, 1075, 1248) m Yellow

Dog's sweater: 110 (250, 400) yd/100 (228, 365) m Yellow

Needles sizes 6, 8 US (8, 6 UK; 4, 5 mm), *or size needed to obtain gauge*

Circular needle size 6 US (8 UK, 4 mm), 16 in./40 cm long

Double-pointed needles (dpn) size 8 US (6 UK, 5 mm)

Cable needle (cn)

Stitch holders and stitch markers

■ Gauge

26 sts and 26 rows = 4 in./10 cm in cable pat using larger needles

Always check gauge to save time and ensure correct yardage and correct fit! Always measure your child!

■ Cable Pattern (multiple of 8 sts plus 2 extra)

Row 1 (RS): P2, *k6, p2; rep from *.

Row 2 and all WS rows:
K the k sts and p the p sts.

Row 3: P2, *sl 3 sts to cn and hold to back of work, k3, k3 from cn, p2; rep from *.

Rows 5 and 7: Rep row 1.

Row 8: Rep row 2.

Rep rows 1–8 for cable pat.

CHILD'S SWEATER

■ Back

With smaller needles, cast on 58 (66, 72, 78, 86, 92, 100) sts. Work in k1, p1 rib for 1 (1, 1, 1, 1.5, 1.5, 1.5) in./2.5 (2.5, 2.5, 2.5, 4, 4, 4) cm, inc 8 (8, 10, 12, 12, 14, 14) sts evenly across last WS row to 66 (74, 82, 90, 98, 106, 114) sts. Change to larger needles. Work in cable pat until piece measures 10 (11, 13, 16, 17.5, 19, 20.5) in./25.5 (28, 33, 40.5, 44.5, 48, 52) cm from beg. Place 18 (22, 25, 29, 32, 35, 38) sts on a holder for one shoulder, place next 30 (30, 32, 32, 34, 36, 38) sts on a 2nd holder for back neck, place rem 18 (22, 25, 29, 32, 35, 38) sts on a 3rd holder for other shoulder.

■ Front

Work as for back until piece measures 8 (9, 11, 13.5, 15, 16.5, 18) in./20 (23, 28, 34, 38, 42, 45.5) cm from beg.

Neck shaping: *Next row (RS):* Work 24 (28, 31, 35, 39, 42, 45) sts, join 2nd ball of yarn and bind off center 18 (18, 20, 20, 20, 22, 24) sts, work to end. Working both sides at same time, bind off from each neck edge 2 sts twice, 1 st 2 (2, 2, 2, 3, 3, 3) times. Work even until same length as back. Place rem 18 (22, 25, 29, 32, 35, 38) sts each side on holders for later finishing.

Shoulder seams: *With wrong sides facing each other,* place sts for both right shoulders on 2 parallel dpn. With a 3rd dpn, k through 1st st on each needle, then the 2nd st on each needle, and pass 1st over 2nd to bind off. Cont in this way to end for a knitted seam. Work in same way for left shoulder seam.

■ Sleeves

Place markers on front and back 5 (5.5, 6, 6.5, 7, 7.5, 8) in./12.5 (14, 15.5, 16.5, 18, 19, 20.5) cm down from shoulder seams for armholes. With RS facing, pick up and k 66 (72, 78, 84, 92, 98, 104) sts between markers. **Est cable pat:** *Next row (WS):* P0 (3, 2, 1, 1, 0, 3), k2, [p6, k2] 8 (8, 9, 10, 11, 12, 12) times, p0 (3, 2, 1, 1, 0, 3). Cont in pat as est for 4 rows more, then dec 1 st each side every 4th row 2 (3, 3, 9, 10, 14, 16) times, every other row 11 (12, 13, 9,

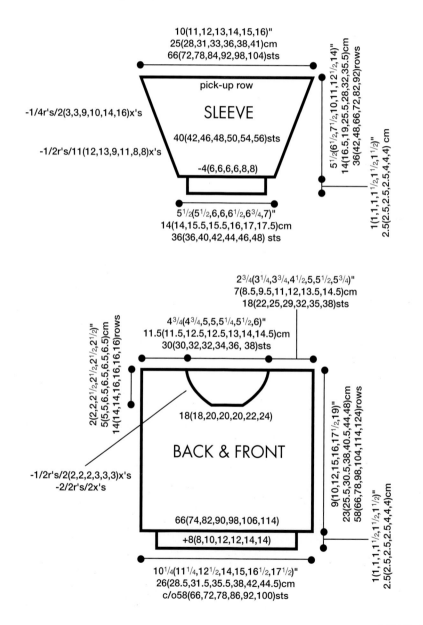

10(11,12,13,14,15,16)"
25(28,31,33,36,38,41)cm
66(72,78,84,92,98,104)sts

pick-up row

SLEEVE

40(42,46,48,50,54,56)sts

-4(6,6,6,6,8,8)

-1/4r's/2(3,3,9,10,14,16)x's

-1/2r's/11(12,13,9,11,8,8)x's

5¹/2(6¹/2,7¹/2,10,11,12¹/2,14)"
14(16.5,19,25.5,28,32,35.5)cm
36(42,48,66,72,82,92)rows

1(1,1,1,1¹/2,1¹/2)"
2.5(2.5,2.5,2.5,4,4,4) cm

5¹/2(5¹/2,6,6,6¹/2,6³/4,7)"
14(14,15.5,15.5,16,17,17.5)cm
36(36,40,42,44,46,48) sts

2³/4(3¹/4,3³/4,4¹/2,5,5¹/2,5³/4)"
7(8.5,9.5,11,12,13.5,14.5)cm
18(22,25,29,32,35,38)sts

4³/4(4³/4,5,5,5¹/4,5¹/2,6)"
11.5(11.5,12.5,12.5,13,14,14.5)cm
30(30,32,32,34,36, 38)sts

2(2,2,2¹/2,2,2¹/2,2¹/2)"
5(5,5,6.5,6.5,6.5,6.5)cm
14(14,14,16,16,16,16)rows

18(18,20,20,20,22,24)

BACK & FRONT

9(10,12,15,16,17,19)"
23(25.5,30.5,38,40.5,44,48)cm
58(66,78,98,104,114,124)rows

-1/2r's/2(2,2,2,3,3,3)x's
-2/2r's/2x's

66(74,82,90,98,106,114)

+8(8,10,12,12,14,14)

1(1,1,1,1¹/2,1¹/2)"
2.5(2.5,2.5,2.5,4,4,4)cm

10¹/4(11¹/4,12¹/2,14,15,16¹/2,17¹/2)"
26(28.5,31.5,35.5,38,42,44.5)cm
c/o58(66,72,78,86,92,100)sts

11, 8, 8) times, to 40 (42, 46, 48, 50, 54, 56) sts. Cont in pat until sleeve measures 5.5 (6.5, 7.5, 10, 11, 12.5, 14) in./14 (16.5, 19, 25.5, 28, 32, 35.5) cm, dec 4 (6, 6, 6, 6, 8, 8) sts evenly across last row, to 36 (36, 40, 42, 44, 46, 48) sts. Change to smaller needles and work 1 (1, 1, 1, 1.5, 1.5, 1.5) in./2.5 (2.5, 2.5, 2.5, 4, 4, 4) cm in k1, p1 rib. Bind off loosely and evenly in rib.

■ Finishing

For neckband, with circular needle, pick up and k 74 (74, 78, 78, 82, 86, 90) sts evenly around neck. Join and work in k1, p1 rib for 1.75 in./4.5 cm. Bind off loosely and evenly in rib. Sew side and sleeve seams.

DOG'S SWEATER

With smaller needles, cast on 91 (95, 101) sts for neck and work in k1, p1 rib for 1.5 (2, 3) in./4 (5, 7.5) cm, inc 23 (27, 37) sts evenly across last (WS) row, to 114 (122, 138) sts. Change to larger needles. Work in cable pat until piece measures 3 (4, 4.5) in./8 (10, 11.5) cm from beg, end with a WS row.

Split for leg opening: *Next row (RS):* Work 13 sts and place rem sts on a holder. Cont on these 13 sts only (working last 3 sts in St st instead of twisting cable) for 3 (3.5, 3.5) in./7.5 (9, 9) cm, end with a WS row. Place sts on a 2nd holder. Bind off next 12 sts from the 1st holder for leg opening, then work next 64 (72, 88) sts only for 3 (3.5, 3.5) in./7.5 (9, 9) cm, end with a WS row. Place sts on the 2nd holder. Bind off next 12 sts from the 1st holder for leg opening, then

work rem 13 sts (working 1st 3 sts in St st instead of twisting cable) for 3 (3.5, 3.5) in./7.5 (9, 9) cm, end with a WS row. *Next row (RS):* Work 13 sts from the 2nd holder, cast on 12 sts, work 64 (72, 88) sts from the 2nd holder, cast on 12 sts, work rem 13 sts from needle. Cont on all sts until piece measures 6.5 (9, 13) in./16.5 (23, 33) cm, or desired length from beg.

Tail shaping: Bind off 0 (15, 19) sts at beg of next 0 (2, 2) rows. Dec 1 st each side every other row 3 (4, 8) times, every row 10 (16, 16) times. Bind off 0 (4, 4) sts at beg of next 4 rows, 0 (5, 5) sts at beg of next 2 rows. Bind off rem 88 (26, 26) sts.

■ Finishing

Sew center seam, leaving 1.5 in./4 cm open at neck opening.

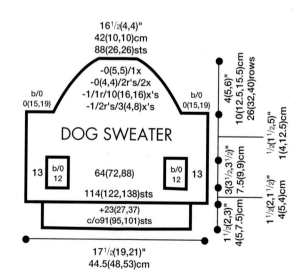

School Days

Shawl-collared, knit in bulky weight yarn, this double-breasted classic jacket with buttons will make Grandfather jealous. A QuickKnit™ with class, this is perfect to wear to school or on a pumpkin hunt.

■ Sizes

2 (4, 6, 8) Years

Finished chest (buttoned): 26.5 (28.5, 30.75, 33) in./65.5 (70.5, 76, 82.5) cm

Length, shoulder to hem: 13 (14.5, 16, 18) in./32.5 (36.5, 40.5, 45.5) cm

■ Materials

Bulky weight wool *that will obtain gauge below*

470 (560, 700, 835) yd/425 (510, 635, 760) m Purple

Needles sizes 8, 9 (6, 5 UK; 5, 5.5 mm), *or size needed to obtain gauge*

Double-pointed needles (dpn) size 9 US (5 UK, 5.5 mm)

Four (4, 6, 6) 1 in./2.5 cm buttons, stitch holders, and stitch markers

■ Gauge

16 sts and 22 rows = 4 in./10 cm in St st using larger needles; 20 sts and 22 rows = 4 in./10 cm in k1, p2 rib using larger needles

Always check gauge to save time and ensure correct yardage and correct fit! Always measure your child!

Sample in photographs knit in Rowan Chunky Wool #887 Bilberry.

■ Back

With smaller straight needles, cast on 52 (56, 61, 66) sts and work in k1, p1 rib for 1.25 (1.25, 1.5, 1.5) in./3 (3, 4, 4) cm. Change to larger needles and work in St st until piece measures 13 (14.5, 16, 18) in./32.5 (36.5, 40.5, 45.5) cm from beg. Work 17 (19, 21, 23) sts and place on a holder for one shoulder for later finishing, bind off next 18 (18, 19, 20) sts for back neck, work last 17 (19, 21, 23) sts and place on a holder for 2nd shoulder for later finishing.

■ Left front

With smaller straight needles, cast on 41 (43, 45, 47) sts and work as foll: *Next row (RS):* Work in k1, p1 rib over first 17 (19, 21, 23) sts, [p2, k1] 8 times. *Next row (WS):* K3, [p1, k2] 7 times, cont k1, p1 rib to end. Rep last 2 rows until 1.25 (1.25, 1.5, 1.5) in./3 (3, 4, 4) cm from beg, end with a WS row. Change to larger needles. *Next row (RS):* Work 17 (19, 21, 23) sts in St st, work rem 24 sts in rib as est, working 2 button- holes as foll: Rib 3 sts, bind off 2 p sts, rib to last 4 sts, bind off 2 p sts, work to end. *Next row:* Cast on 2 sts over bound-off sts. Cont working 1 (1, 2, 2) more set of buttonholes spaced 3.5 in./9 cm apart. Work even until

same length as back. Place 17 (19, 21, 23) shoulder sts on a holder and cont rib band on 24 sts for 2.25 (2.25, 2.5, 2.5) in./5.5 (5.5, 6.5, 6.5) cm more, end with a WS row.

Collar shaping: Bind off 8 sts at beg of next RS row, and cont to bind off from same edge 8 sts twice more.

■ Right front

Work as for left front, reversing rib band and collar shaping and omitting buttonholes.

Shoulder seams: *With wrong sides facing* *each other,* place sts of back and front right shoulders on 2 parallel dpn. With a 3rd dpn, k through 1st st on each needle, then through the 2nd st on each needle, and pass 1st over 2nd to bind off. Cont in this way to end for a knitted seam. Work in same way for left shoulder seam.

■ Sleeves

Place markers on front and back 6 (6.5, 7, 7.5) in./15 (16.5, 18, 19) cm down from shoulder seam. With RS facing and larger needles, pick up and k 48 (52, 56, 60) sts

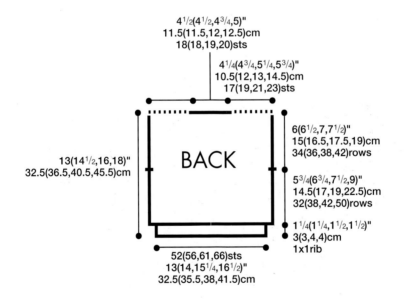

4¹/₂(4¹/₂,4³/₄,5)"
11.5(11.5,12,12.5)cm
18(18,19,20)sts

4¹/₄(4³/₄,5¹/₄,5³/₄)"
10.5(12,13,14.5)cm
17(19,21,23)sts

BACK

13(14¹/₂,16,18)"
32.5(36.5,40.5,45.5)cm

6(6¹/₂,7,7¹/₂)"
15(16.5,17.5,19)cm
34(36,38,42)rows

5³/₄(6³/₄,7¹/₂,9)"
14.5(17,19,22.5)cm
32(38,42,50)rows

1¹/₄(1¹/₄,1¹/₂,1¹/₂)"
3(3,4,4)cm
1x1rib

52(56,61,66)sts
13(14,15¹/₄,16¹/₂)"
32.5(35.5,38,41.5)cm

between markers. Work in St st, dec 1 st each side every 4th row 11 (12, 12, 11) times, every 6th row 0 (0, 2, 4) times, to 26 (28, 28, 30) sts. Work even until sleeve measures 8.75 (9.75, 12, 13.5) in./22 (24.5, 30, 34) cm. Change to smaller needles and work in k1, p1 rib for 1.25 (1.25, 1.5, 1.5) in./3 (3, 4, 4) cm. Bind off in rib.

■ Finishing

Sew sleeve and side seams. Sew shaped edges of collar tog so that the seam will not show when collar is folded to the right side. Sew straight edge of collar to back neck. Sew buttons on right front opposite buttonholes.

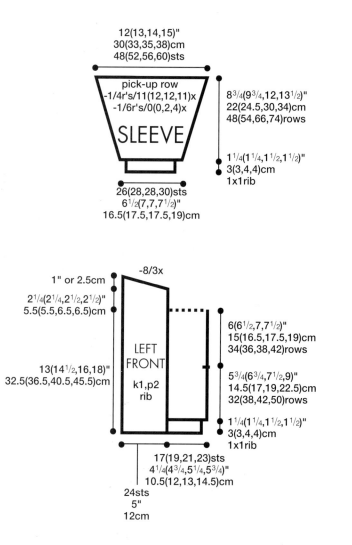

12(13,14,15)"
30(33,35,38)cm
48(52,56,60)sts

pick-up row
-1/4r's/11(12,12,11)x
-1/6r's/0(0,2,4)x

SLEEVE

8³/4(9³/4,12,13¹/2)"
22(24.5,30,34)cm
48(54,66,74)rows

1¹/4(1¹/4,1¹/2,1¹/2)"
3(3,4,4)cm
1x1rib

26(28,28,30)sts
6¹/2(7,7,7¹/2)"
16.5(17.5,17.5,19)cm

-8/3x

1" or 2.5cm

2¹/4(2¹/4,2¹/2,2¹/2)"
5.5(5.5,6.5,6.5)cm

LEFT
FRONT

k1,p2
rib

6(6¹/2,7,7¹/2)"
15(16.5,17.5,19)cm
34(36,38,42)rows

13(14¹/2,16,18)"
32.5(36.5,40.5,45.5)cm

5³/4(6³/4,7¹/2,9)"
14.5(17,19,22.5)cm
32(38,42,50)rows

1¹/4(1¹/4,1¹/2,1¹/2)"
3(3,4,4)cm
1x1rib

17(19,21,23)sts
4¹/4(4³/4,5¹/4,5³/4)"
10.5(12,13,14.5)cm

24sts
5"
12cm

Button, Button

Another darling learn-to-knit or beginner QuickKnit™ project, this soft, rich bulky cotton chenille double-breasted sweater jacket is a showstopper. Use any bright buttons you can find for offbeat style; I like to use circles and squares and triangles all together. When you're working with chenille, remember always to pull the yarn evenly and closely, as chenille can bubble on the back.

■ Sizes

3 Months (6 Months, 1, 2, 3 Years)

Sweater finished chest: 19 (21, 23, 25, 27) in./48 (53, 58, 63.5, 68.5) cm

Sweater length, shoulder to hem: 9 (10, 11.5, 12, 13) in./23 (25.5, 29, 30.5, 33) cm

Beanie, circumference: Newborn, 15 in./39 cm; Small, 17 in./44 cm; Medium, 18.5 in./46 cm

■ Materials

100% cotton chenille *that will obtain gauge below*

Sweater: 185 (225, 275, 325, 385) yd/170 (210, 250, 300, 320) m Navy or Rose

Beanie: 54 (60, 72) yd/50 (55, 66) m Navy or Rose

Tassel: 25 yd/23 m 100% cotton

Straight needles and double-pointed needles (dpn) size 6 US (UK 8, 4 mm), *or size needed to obtain gauge*

Eight ⅝ in./1.5 cm buttons in various contrasting colors and shapes, stitch holders, and stitch markers

■ Gauge

16 sts and 20 rows = 4 in./10 cm in St st using size 6 needles

Always check gauge to save time and ensure correct yardage and correct fit! Always measure your child!

Sample in studio photograph knit in Crystal Palace Chenille #6246 Blue Violet; sample in location photograph (page 107) knit in Rowan Cotton Chenille #377 Raspberry.

SWEATER

■ Back

With straight needles, cast on 38 (42, 46, 50, 54) sts. Work in garter st 4 rows. Work in St st until piece measures 9 (10, 11.5, 12, 13) in./23 (25.5, 29, 30.5, 33) cm from beg. *Next RS row:* Work 11 (12, 14, 15, 16) sts for one shoulder and place on a holder, work 16 (18, 18, 20, 22) sts for back neck and place on a 2nd holder, work rem 11 (12, 14, 15, 16) sts for 2nd shoulder and place on a 3rd holder.

■ Left front

With straight needles, cast on 28 (30, 32, 34, 36) sts. K 4 rows. Work in St st, but always k first 4 sts on WS for front edge, until piece measures 7 (8, 9.5, 9.5, 10.5) in./17.5 (20.5, 24, 24, 26.5) cm from beg, ending with RS row.

Neck shaping: Bind off 13 (14, 14, 14, 15) sts at beg next WS row (neck edge) and cont to dec 1 st at neck edge every other row 4 (4, 4, 5, 5) times. Work even, if necessary, until same length as back. Place rem 11 (12, 14, 15, 16) sts on a holder for later finishing.

■ Right front

Work as for left front, working buttonholes after piece measures 3.5 (4, 4.5, 5, 5.5) in./9 (10, 11.5, 12.5, 14) cm from beg, ending with WS row. *Next RS row:* Work buttonhole row as foll: K4, k2tog, yo, k8, k2tog, yo, work to end. Work another buttonhole row at 6.5 (7.5, 8.5, 9.5, 10.5) in./16.5 (19, 22, 24, 27) cm from beg. Work even until piece measures 7 (8, 9.5, 9.5, 10.5) in./17.5 (20.5, 24, 24, 26.5) cm from beg, ending with a WS row. Work as for left front, reversing neck shaping.

Shoulder seams: *With wrong sides facing each other,* place sts of back and front right shoulders on 2 parallel dpn. With a 3rd dpn, k through 1st st on each needle, then through the 2nd st on each needle, and pass 1st over 2nd to bind off. Cont in this way to end for a knitted seam. Work in same way for left shoulder seam.

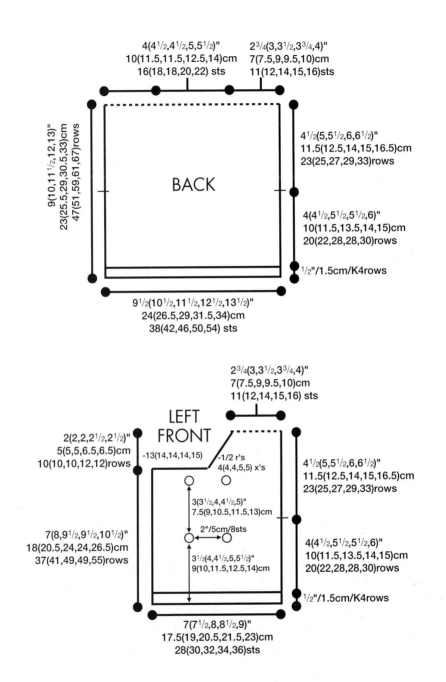

4(4½,4½,5,5½)"
10(11.5,11.5,12.5,14)cm
16(18,18,20,22) sts

2¾(3,3½,3¾,4)"
7(7.5,9,9.5,10)cm
11(12,14,15,16)sts

9(10,11½,12,13)"
23(25.5,29,30.5,33)cm
47(51,59,61,67)rows

BACK

4½(5,5½,6,6½)"
11.5(12.5,14,15,16.5)cm
23(25,27,29,33)rows

4(4½,5½,5½,6)"
10(11.5,13.5,14,15)cm
20(22,28,28,30)rows

½"/1.5cm/K4rows

9½(10½,11½,12½,13½)"
24(26.5,29,31.5,34)cm
38(42,46,50,54) sts

2¾(3,3½,3¾,4)"
7(7.5,9,9.5,10)cm
11(12,14,15,16) sts

LEFT
FRONT

2(2,2,2½,2½)"
5(5,5,6.5,6.5)cm
10(10,10,12,12)rows

-13(14,14,14,15)
-1/2 r's
4(4,4,5,5) x's

4½(5,5½,6,6½)"
11.5(12.5,14,15,16.5)cm
23(25,27,29,33)rows

3(3½,4,4½,5)"
7.5(9,10.5,11.5,13)cm

2"/5cm/8sts

7(8,9½,9½,10½)"
18(20.5,24,24,26.5)cm
37(41,49,49,55)rows

4(4½,5½,5½,6)"
10(11.5,13.5,14,15)cm
20(22,28,28,30)rows

3½(4,4½,5,5½)"
9(10,11.5,12.5,14)cm

½"/1.5cm/K4rows

7(7½,8,8½,9)"
17.5(19,20.5,21.5,23)cm
28(30,32,34,36)sts

■ Sleeves

Place markers on front and back 4.5 (5, 5.5, 6, 6.5) in./11.5 (12.5, 14, 15, 16.5) cm down from shoulder seams for armholes. With RS facing and straight needles, pick up and k 36 (40, 44, 48, 52) sts between markers. Work in St st for 5 rows, then dec 1 st each end on next row, then every 4th row 4 (5, 5, 5, 5) times more, then every other row 0 (0 ,0, 1, 2) times, to 26 (28, 32, 34, 36) sts. Work even until piece measures 4.5 (5, 5, 5.5, 6) in./11.5 (12.5, 12.5, 14, 15) cm from beg, ending with RS row. K 4 rows, and bind off loosely purlwise.

■ Finishing

Sew sleeve and side seams. With RS facing, pick up and k 1 st in every st and row evenly around neck edge. Work in garter st for 3 rows, and bind off loosely purlwise. Sew buttons opposite buttonholes.

BEANIE

With straight needles, cast on 64 (72, 80) sts. Work in St st (k on RS, p on WS) for 6 rows, inc 8 sts in last row, to 72 (80, 88) sts. Work even for 4.5 (4.5, 5) in./11.5 (11.5, 13) cm.

■ Shape crown

Next row (RS): [K2tog, k8] 7 (8, 8) times. K2tog 1 (0, 0) time, k to end, 64 (72, 80) sts. P 1 row. *Next row:* [K2tog, k2] 16 (18, 20) times, 48 (54, 60) sts. P 1 row. K2tog across, cut 9 in./23 cm tail, and pull through.

■ Finishing

Sew back seam, reversing seam for rolled edge. Make 2 pleats 4 in./10 cm apart, centered in front, and sew 2 buttons on each pleat. With cotton yarn, make tassel by winding around 3 in./7.5 cm cardboard rectangle. Remove cardboard, and tie 9 in./23 cm length through, pulling very tight. Tie another length of yarn 1 in./2.5 cm from first knot. Cut ends and trim evenly. Using the 9 in./23 cm tail, sew firmly to cap top.

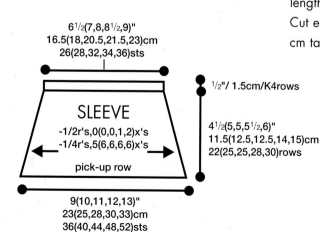

6½(7,8,8½,9)"
16.5(18,20.5,21.5,23)cm
26(28,32,34,36)sts

SLEEVE

-1/2r's,0(0,0,1,2)x's
-1/4r's,5(6,6,6,6)x's

pick-up row

½"/ 1.5cm/K4rows

4½(5,5,5½,6)"
11.5(12.5,12.5,14,15)cm
22(25,25,28,30)rows

9(10,11,12,13)"
23(25,28,30,33)cm
36(40,44,48,52)sts

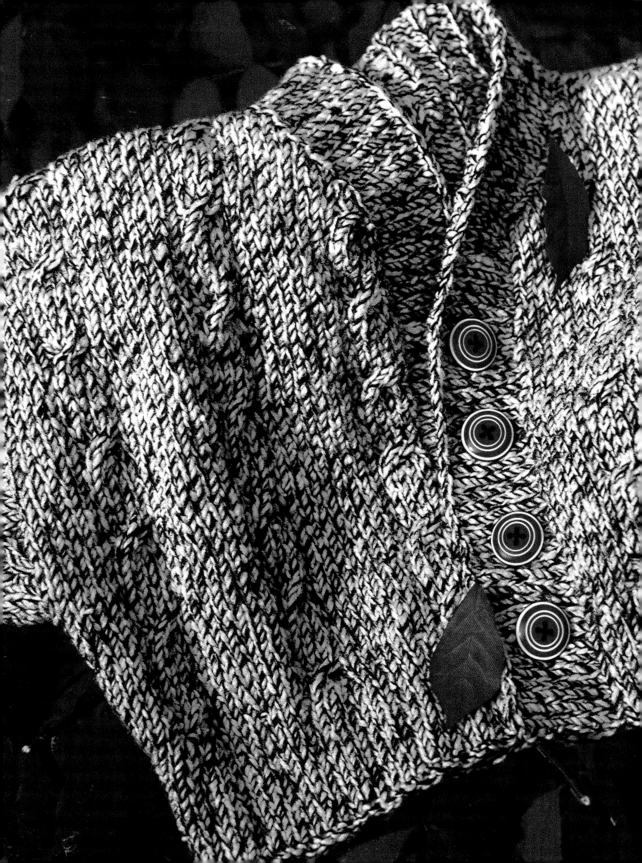

Hum Bug

The cardigan sweater with a five-button front has matching pantaloons in the same tweed wool with a subtle cable, a very light yet warm ensemble for cool autumn play. Also try it in a solid-color yarn to emphasize the easy cables.

■ Sizes
2 (3, 4) Years

Sweater finished chest (buttoned): 26.75 (28.25, 30.5) in./67 (70.5, 76) cm

Sweater length, shoulder to waistband: 10 (12, 14) in./25 (30.5, 35) cm

Pants, waist to ankle: 16 (17.75, 19.5) in./40.5 (45, 49.5) cm

■ Materials
DK wool *that will obtain gauge below*

874 (1050, 1292) yd/770 (955, 1175) m Black and White Tweed

Straight needles and double-pointed needles (dpn) size 5 US (9 UK, 3.75 mm), *or size needed to obtain gauge*

Circular needle size 5 US (9 UK, 3.75 mm), 24 in./60 cm long

Cable needle (cn)

Sample in photographs knit in Rowan DK Marl Wool #823 Humbug.

Five (6, 6) 5/8 in./1.5 cm buttons, .5 yd/ .5 m elastic, stitch holders, and stitch markers

■ Gauge
27 sts and 30 rows = 4 in./10 cm in cable pat using size 5 needles

Always check gauge to save time and ensure correct yardage and correct fit! Always measure your child!

■ Rib Pattern

K3, p1 rib (multiple of 4 sts plus 1)

Row 1 (RS): P1, *k3, p1; rep from *.

Row 2: K the k sts and p the p sts.

Rep row 2 for k3, p1 rib.

■ Cable Pattern (multiple of 14 sts plus 6)

Row 1 (RS): *P1, k4, p1, k8; rep from *, end p1, k4, p1.

Row 2 and all WS rows through row 10: K the k sts and p the p sts.

Row 3: *P1, sl next 2 sts to cn and hold in back of work, k2, k2 from cn (cable), p1, k8; rep from *, end p1, work cable, p1.

Rows 5, 7, and 9: Rep row 1.

Rep rows 1–10 for cable pat.

SWEATER

■ Back

With straight needles, cast on 81 (89, 97) sts. Work in k3, p1 rib for 2 (2.5, 3) in./5 (6.5, 7.5) cm, inc 9 (7, 7) sts evenly across last row, to 90 (96, 104) sts. **Beg cable pat:** *Next row (RS):* K0 (3, 0), work cable to last 0 (3, 0) sts, k0 (3, 0). Cont in pat as est until piece measures 10 (12, 14) in./25 (30.5, 35) cm from beg. *Next RS row:* Work 29 (30, 32) sts for one shoulder and place on a holder, work 32 (36, 40) sts for back neck and place on a 2nd holder, work rem 29 (30, 32) sts for 2nd shoulder and place on a 3rd holder for later finishing.

■ Left front

With straight needles, cast on 37 (41, 45) sts. Work in rib as for back, inc 3 (1, 0) sts in last row, to 40 (42, 45) sts. **Beg cable pat:** *Next row (RS):* K0 (2, 5), work cable to last 6 sts, k6. Cont in pat as est until piece measures 8 (10, 12) in./20.5 (25.5, 30) cm from beg, ending with a RS row.

Neck shaping: Bind off 3 sts at beg next WS row (neck edge) and cont to bind off from neck edge 3 sts 0 (0, 1) time more, 2 sts 2 (3, 2) times. Dec 1 st every other row 4 (3, 3) times. Work even, if necessary, until same length as back. Place rem 29 (30, 32) sts on a holder for later finishing.

■ Right front

Work as for left front, reversing neck shaping.
Shoulder seams: *With wrong sides facing each other,* place sts of back and front right shoulders on 2 parallel dpn. With a 3rd dpn, k through 1st st on each needle, then through the 2nd st on each needle, and pass 1st over 2nd to bind off. Cont in this way to end for a knitted seam. Work in same way for left shoulder seam.

■ Sleeves

Place markers on front and back 6 (6.75, 7.25) in./15 (17, 18) cm from shoulder seams for armholes. With RS facing, pick up and k 82 (92, 98) sts between markers. Beg on row 10 of cable pat, and work as foll: *Next row (WS):* P3 (1, 4), work cable pat to last 3 (1, 4) sts, p3 (1, 4). Cont in pat as est for 1 in./2.5 cm, then dec 1 st each end on next row, then every other row 15 (18, 19) times more, to 50 (54, 58) sts. Work even until piece measures 5 (5.25, 5.75) in./12.5 (13, 14.5) cm from pick-up row, dec 1 st on last row, to 49 (53, 57) sts. Work in k3, p1 rib for 1.5 in./4 cm. Bind off loosely and evenly in rib.

■ Button band

With RS facing, pick up and k 72 (90, 108) sts along right front, work 33 (37, 41) sts of back neck, pick up and k 72 (90, 108) sts along left front for a total of 177 (217, 257) sts. Work in k3, p1 rib for 1.5 in./4 cm, AT THE SAME TIME, after .5 in./1.5 cm, work 5 (6, 6) evenly spaced buttonholes on left front, every 1.5 (1.5, 2) in./4 (4, 5) cm from bottom, by k2tog, yo for each buttonhole. Bind off firmly and evenly in rib. Sew on buttons.

PANTS

■ Legs (make 2)

*With straight needles, cast on 105 (117, 133) sts. Work in k3, p1 rib for 2 (2.5, 3) in./5 (6.5, 7.5) cm. Inc 7 (9, 7) sts evenly across last WS row, to 112 (126, 140) sts. Work in cable pat until piece measures 8 (8.5, 9) in./20 (21.5, 22.5) cm above cuff. Rep from * for second leg.

Crotch shaping: Bind off 3 sts at beg next 2 rows. Dec 1 st each end every other row 4 times, to 98 (112, 126) sts.

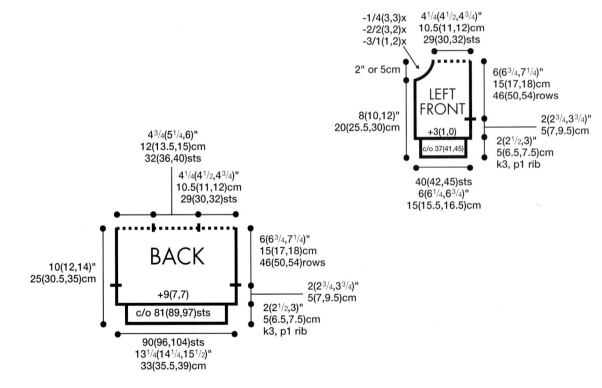

■ Pant body

Place both legs on circular needle, total 196 (224, 252) sts. Join, and place marker for beg rnd. Cont in cable pat for 13 (14, 15) in./33 (35.5, 38) cm above cuff. K next rnd, dec 74 (98, 120) sts evenly around, to 122 (126, 132) sts. K 8 (10, 12) rnds. P 1 rnd. K 7 (9, 11) rnds. Place sts on yarn for later finishing.

■ Finishing

Sew crotch and leg seams. Place elastic under waistband and sew live sts to inside waistband. With dpn, cast on 6 sts. K 1 row. Slide sts to other end of needle and k6. Rep last row for I-cord for 7 in./18 cm. Cast off. Thread cord through center of front band of pants and tie.

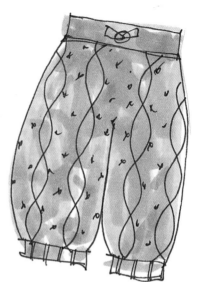

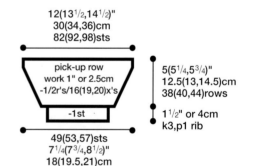

12(13½,14½)"
30(34,36)cm
82(92,98)sts

pick-up row
work 1" or 2.5cm
-1/2r's/16(19,20)x's

-1st

5(5¼,5¾)"
12.5(13,14.5)cm
38(40,44)rows

1½" or 4cm
k3,p1 rib

49(53,57)sts
7¼(7¾,8½)"
18(19.5,21)cm

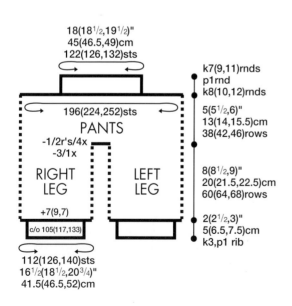

18(18½,19½)"
45(46.5,49)cm
122(126,132)sts

PANTS

196(224,252)sts

-1/2r's/4x
-3/1x

RIGHT LEG

LEFT LEG

+7(9,7)

c/o 105(117,133)

112(126,140)sts
16½(18½,20¾)"
41.5(46.5,52)cm

k7(9,11)rnds
p1rnd
k8(10,12)rnds

5(5½,6)"
13(14,15.5)cm
38(42,46)rows

8(8½,9)"
20(21.5,22.5)cm
60(64,68)rows

2(2½,3)"
5(6.5,7.5)cm
k3,p1 rib

One-Button Vest

Color-blocking is a simple way for beginners to knit a very colorful piece using only one color at a time. With its seed-stitch front and back tabs and buttons, this wool vest is a good QuickKnit™ project.

■ Sizes

4 (6, 8) Years

Finished chest (closed): 23 (26, 29) in./58 (65.5, 73.5) cm

Length, shoulder to hem: 12 (13.5, 15) in./30 (34, 37.5) cm

■ Materials

DK weight wool *that will obtain gauge below*

220 (280, 345) yd/200 (255, 315) m Blue (MC)

132 (170, 210) yd/120 (155, 190) m Green (A)

35 yd/32 m each Purple (B) and Violet (C)

Straight needles and double-pointed needles (dpn) size 5 US (9 UK, 3.75 mm), *or size needed to obtain gauge*

Two .75 in./2 cm buttons and stitch holders

■ Gauge

24 sts and 32 rows = 4 in./10 cm in St st using size 5 needles

Always check gauge to save time and ensure correct yardage and correct fit! Always measure your child!

Sample in photograph knit in Rowan Lightweight DK Wool #125 (MC), #075 (A), #126 (B), and #501 (C).

■ Seed Stitch (over any number of sts)

Row 1 (RS): *K1, p1; rep from * to end.

Row 2: K the p sts and p the k sts.

Rep row 2 for seed st.

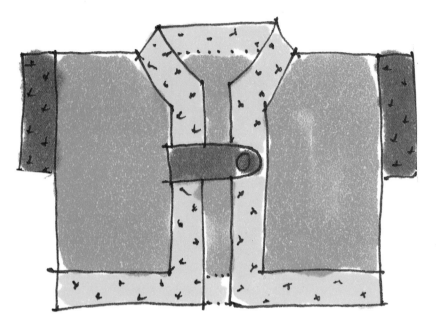

■ Back

With A, cast on 69 (78, 87) sts. Work in seed st for 1 in./2.5 cm. Change to MC and work in St st (k on RS, p on WS) until piece measures 6 (7, 8) in./15 (17.5, 20) cm from beg.

Shape armhole: Bind off 2 (3, 3) sts at beg of next 2 rows. Dec 1 st each side every other row 4 (4, 6) times, to 57 (64, 69) sts. Work even until armhole measures 5 (5.5, 6) in./12.5 (14, 15) cm.

Neck shaping: *Next row:* Work 22 (25, 26) sts, join a 2nd skein of yarn and bind off center 13 (14, 17) sts, work to end. Working both sides at once, bind off from each neck edge 3 sts twice, 2 sts once. Place rem 14 (17, 18) sts from each side on holders for shoulders.

■ Left front

With A, cast on 39 (44, 48) sts. Work in seed st for 1 in./2.5 cm. Change to MC and work in St st, keeping 9 sts at front edge (end of RS rows, beg of WS rows) in seed st with A, until same length as back to armhole. Shape armhole at side edge (beg of RS rows) as for back, to 33 (37, 39) sts. Work even until piece measures 10 (11.5, 13) in./25 (29, 32.5) cm from beg, end with a WS row. **Neck shaping:** *Next row (RS):* Work to last 9 sts, place 9 sts on a holder. Work 2 rows even. Bind off 3 (4, 4) sts at beg of next WS row (neck edge), work to end. Cont to bind off from neck edge 2 sts twice, dec 1 st every other row 3 (3, 4) times. When same length as back, place rem 14 (17, 18) sts on a holder for shoulder.

■ Right front

Work to correspond to left front, working 9-st seed st band at beg of RS rows and end of WS rows and reversing all shaping.

Shoulder seams: *With wrong sides facing each other,* place sts of back and front right shoulders on 2 parallel dpn. With a 3rd dpn and MC, k through 1st st on each needle, then through the 2nd st on each needle, pass 1st over 2nd to bind off. Cont in this way to end for a knitted seam. Work in same way for left shoulder seam.

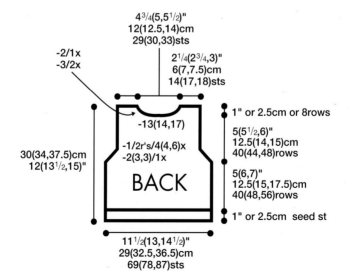

■ Finishing

Neckband: With RS facing and A, beg at right front neck, work in seed st across 9 sts on holder, pick up and k 48 (50, 56) sts evenly around neck edge, work seed st across 9 sts on holder. Work in seed st on all sts for 1 in./2.5 cm. Bind off.

Armhole bands: With RS facing and B, pick up and k 58 (64, 68) sts evenly around each armhole edge. Work in seed st for 1 in./2.5 cm. Bind off. Sew side and armhole band seams.

Front tab: With C, cast on 10 sts. Work in seed st for 2.5 in./6.5 cm. *Next buttonhole row:* Work 4 sts, bind off 2 sts, work to end. *Next row:* Cast on 2 sts over bound-off sts. Dec 1 st each end every row until there are 2 sts. K2tog and fasten off. Sew cast-on edge of tab to right front, just inside of seed st band and approx 2.5 in./6.5 cm down from neck edge, or where desired. Sew button to center of left front seed st band opposite buttonhole.

Back tab: Work as for front tab, omitting buttonhole. Sew tab to center of back and sew button in center of point of tab.

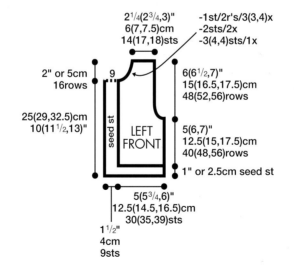

2¼(2¾,3)"
6(7,7.5)cm
14(17,18)sts

-1st/2r's/3(3,4)x
-2sts/2x
-3(4,4)sts/1x

2" or 5cm
16rows

9

6(6½,7)"
15(16.5,17.5)cm
48(52,56)rows

25(29,32.5)cm
10(11½,13)"

seed st

LEFT FRONT

5(6,7)"
12.5(15,17.5)cm
40(48,56)rows

1" or 2.5cm seed st

5(5¾,6)"
12.5(14.5,16.5)cm
30(35,39)sts

1½"
4cm
9sts

■ Snowbound outings, solstice celebra-

tions, and sparkling air challenge our wits

and nip our noses as we head into winter.

Everything from thick luscious wools to velvety chenille

feels soft in our nimble fingers, and rich, pure colors form

the winter palette. I also love bright cotton for inside win-

ter wear, or for winter climates less snowy than mine in

New England. Winter gives you the time to try more com-

plex projects, from the rich Fair Isle tunic to the easy but

unusual cables on the skating sweater. There are still plenty

of QuickKnits™ too, like the simple Aran pullover or my

knit-from-the-top beanie, which is perfect for everyone on

your holiday gift list.

Twirl

Worked in DK wool, doubled, this warm cropped sweater presents an unusual cable. Reminiscent of days gone by, it is finished with a removable loop-stitch collar and cuffs, and crocheted buttons imitating the bobbles.

■ Sizes

2 (4, 6) Years

Finished chest (buttoned): 28.5 (30, 33) in./72 (77.5, 83) cm

Length, shoulder to hem: 11 (14, 15.5) in./28 (35, 39) cm

■ Materials

DK weight wool *that will obtain gauge below*

1020 (1340, 1610) yd/935 (1225, 1465) m in Green (MC)

DK weight mohair *that will obtain gauge below*

165 (175, 182) yd/150 (160, 165) m in Black (CC)

Needles sizes 6, 7, 8 US (8, 7, 6 UK; 4, 4.5, 5 mm), *or size needed to obtain gauge*

Double-pointed needles (dpn) size 8 US (6 UK, 5 mm)

Sample in photographs knit in Rowan Lightweight DK Wool (double stranded), and Kid Silk in #090 Jade (MC) and #999 Coal (CC).

Crochet hook size F (8 UK, 4 mm)

Cable needle (cn)

Stitch holders and stitch markers

■ Gauge

16 sts and 24 rows = 4 in./10 cm in St st with 2 strands of MC held tog using size 8 needles; 17 sts of cable panel = 2.5 in./6.5 cm wide; 16 sts and 24 rows = 4 in./10 cm in loop st with 2 strands of CC held tog using size 7 needles

Always check gauge to save time and ensure correct yardage and correct fit! Always measure your child!

■ Stitch Patterns

4-st right purl cable (RPC): Sl 1 st to cn and hold to *back,* k3, p1 from cn.

5-st right purl cable (RPC): Sl 2 sts to cn and hold to *back,* k3, p2 from cn.

5-st left purl cable (LPC): Sl 3 sts to cn and hold to *front,* p2, k3 from cn.

7-st right cable (RC): Sl 4 sts to cn and hold to *back,* k3, sl p st from cn to LH needle and p1, k3 from cn.

Make bobble (MB): K into front, back, front, and back of st (4 sts made in 1 st), turn, p4, turn, k4, turn, p2tog twice, turn, k2tog.

■ Cable Panel Pattern (over 17 sts)

Row 1 (WS): P1tbl (through back lp), k4, p3, k1, p3, k4, p1tbl.

Row 2: K1tbl, p4, 7-st RC, p4, k1tbl.

Row 3 and all foll WS rows: K the k sts and p the p sts, and p first and last st tbl.

Row 4: K1tbl, p2, 5-st RPC, p1, 5-st LPC, p2, k1tbl.

Row 6: K1tbl, p2, k3, p2, MB, p2, k3, p2, k1tbl.

Row 8: K1tbl, p9, 4-st RPC, p2, k1tbl.

Row 10: K1tbl, p8, 4-st RPC, p3, k1tbl.

Row 12: K1tbl, p7, 4-st RPC, p4, k1tbl.

Row 14: K1tbl, p6, 4-st RPC, p5, k1tbl.

Row 16: K1tbl, p5, 4-st RPC, p6, k1tbl.

Row 18: K1tbl, p4, 4-st RPC, p7, k1tbl.

Row 20: K1tbl, p3, 4-st RPC, p8, k1tbl.

Row 22: K1tbl, p2, 4-st RPC, p4, k3, p2, k1tbl.

Row 24: Rep row 6.

Row 26: K1tbl, p2, 5-st LPC, p1, 5-st RPC, p2, k1tbl.

Rep rows 1–26 for cable panel.

■ Loop Stitch (over any number of sts)

Row 1 (RS): Knit.

Row 2 (WS): *K next st, wrapping yarn around index and middle fingers to form a loop, but do not sl this st from needle, sl the st just worked back to LH needle and k2tog tbl (through back loop), remove fingers from loop; rep from * in every st.

Row 3: K1tbl in every st.

Row 4: Knit.

Rep rows 1–4 for loop st.

■ Back

With size 6 needles and 2 strands MC held tog, cast on 63 (67, 71) sts. Work in k1, p1 rib for 6 rows, inc 22 (22, 23) sts evenly across last row, to 85 (89, 94) sts. Change to size 8 needles. **Beg pat:** *Next Row (RS):* Work 3 (3, 4) sts in St st, *k1tbl, p4, k3, p1, k3, p4, k1tbl (17 sts cable panel)*, 3 (4, 5) sts in St st, rep between *s once, 5 (7, 8) sts in St st, rep between *s once, 3 (4, 5) sts in St st, rep between *s once, 3 (3, 4) sts in St st. Cont in pat as est until piece measures 11 (14, 15.5) in./28 (35, 39) cm from beg. Work 31 (32, 34) sts and place on a holder for shoulder, bind off next 23 (25, 26) sts for back neck, work to end and place rem 31 (32, 34) sts on a 2nd holder for 2nd shoulder.

■ Left front

With size 6 needles and 2 strands MC held tog, cast on 38 (40, 42) sts. Work in k1, p1 rib as foll: *Next row (RS):* *K1, p1; rep from * to last 2 sts, k2. *Next row:* *K1, p1; rep from * to end. Rep last 2 rows for a total of 6 rows, inc 11 (11, 12) sts evenly across last row as foll: *Inc row (WS):* Rib 7, rib to end inc 11 (11, 12) sts, to 49 (51, 54) sts. Change to size 8 needles. **Beg pat:** *Next row (RS):* Work 2 (3, 4) sts in St st, *k1tbl, p4, k3, p1, k3, p4, k1tbl (17 sts cable panel)*, 3 (4, 5) sts in St st, rep between *s once, 2 (3, 4) sts in St st, work last 7 sts in rib as est for button band. Cont in pat as est until piece measures 9 (12, 13.5) in./23 (30, 34) cm from beg, end with a RS row.

Neck shaping: *Next row (WS):* Rib 7 sts and place on a holder, bind off 1 (2, 3) st (neck edge), work to end. Cont to bind off from

neck edge 3 sts twice, 2 sts twice. Work even until same length as back. Place rem 31 (33, 34) sts on a holder for shoulder. Place markers in center of button band for 4 (5, 5) buttons, the first 1 in./2.5 cm from lower edge, the last 1 in./2.5 cm below 1st neck dec, and 2 (3, 3) others spaced evenly between.

■ Right front

Work to correspond to left front, reversing shaping and working buttonholes in 7-st rib band opposite buttons as foll: Rib 2, bind off 3 sts, rib to end. On next row, cast on 3 sts over bound-off sts.

Shoulder seams: *With wrong sides facing each other,* place sts of front and back right shoulders on 2 parallel dpn. With a 3rd dpn, k through 1st st on each needle, then through the 2nd st on each needle, and pass 1st over 2nd to bind off. Cont in this way to end for a knitted seam. Work left shoulder in same way.

■ Sleeves

Place markers on front and back 5.5 (6, 6.5) in./14 (15, 16.5) cm down from shoulder seams for armholes. With RS facing, size 8 straight needles, and 2 strands MC, pick up and k 51 (55, 59) sts evenly between markers. **Beg pat:** *Next row (WS):* Work 17 (19, 21) sts in St st, p1tbl, k4, p3, k1, p3, k4, p1tbl (17 sts cable panel), 17 (19, 21) sts in St st. Cont in pat as est, dec 1 st each side every 6th row 5 (9, 10) times, every 4th row 3 (0, 0) times, to 35 (37, 39) sts. Work even until sleeve measures 8 (9.5, 10.5) in./20.5

(24, 26.5) cm. Change to size 6 needles and work in k1, p1 rib for 2 in./5 cm. Bind off loosely and evenly in rib.

■ Finishing

With RS facing each other, sew side and sleeve seams.

■ Neckband

With RS facing, size 6 needles, and MC, beg at right front neck edge, rib across 7 sts on holder, pick up and k55 (59, 61) sts evenly around neck edge, rib 7 sts from left front holder. Work in k1, p1 rib for 1 row. Work a buttonhole on right front as before. Cont rib until band measures 1 in./2.5 cm. Bind off in rib.

■ Cuffs

With size 7 needles and 2 strands of CC held tog, cast on 28 (32, 32) sts and work in loop st for 11 rows. Bind off knitwise. Sew cuffs around rib at lower edge of sleeves.

■ Half collar

With size 7 needles and 2 strands of CC held tog, cast on 24 (26, 27) sts and work in loop st for 12 rows. K 3 rows. Bind off knitwise. Work 2nd half of collar in same way. Sew both halves of collar around ribbed neck edge, sewing last 3 k rows to WS of neckband. Sew ends of collar tog at center back neck.

■ Crochet buttons

With 2 strands MC and crochet hook, make a lp on hook, ch 1, 6 sc in lp. *Rnd 2:* 2 sc in each sc, to 12 sc. *Rnd 3:* Dec 1 sc in each sc. Pull through lps tightly to close and pull both ends to underside of button. Make 5 (6, 6) buttons in all and sew to left front, opposite buttonholes.

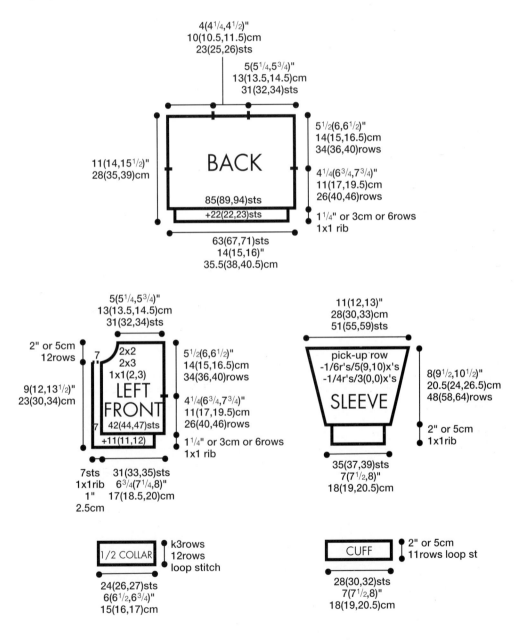

4(4¹/₄,4¹/₂)"
10(10.5,11.5)cm
23(25,26)sts

5(5¹/₄,5³/₄)"
13(13.5,14.5)cm
31(32,34)sts

BACK

5¹/₂(6,6¹/₂)"
14(15,16.5)cm
34(36,40)rows

11(14,15¹/₂)"
28(35,39)cm

4¹/₄(6³/₄,7³/₄)"
11(17,19.5)cm
26(40,46)rows

85(89,94)sts
+22(22,23)sts

1¹/₄" or 3cm or 6rows
1x1 rib

63(67,71)sts
14(15,16)"
35.5(38,40.5)cm

5(5¹/₄,5³/₄)"
13(13.5,14.5)cm
31(32,34)sts

2" or 5cm
12rows

7
2x2
2x3
1x1(2,3)

LEFT FRONT

5¹/₂(6,6¹/₂)"
14(15,16.5)cm
34(36,40)rows

9(12,13¹/₂)"
23(30,34)cm

42(44,47)sts
+11(11,12)

4¹/₄(6³/₄,7³/₄)"
11(17,19.5)cm
26(40,46)rows

7

1¹/₄" or 3cm or 6rows
1x1 rib

7sts
1x1rib
1"
2.5cm

31(33,35)sts
6³/₄(7¹/₄,8)"
17(18.5,20)cm

11(12,13)"
28(30,33)cm
51(55,59)sts

pick-up row
-1/6r's/5(9,10)x's
-1/4r's/3(0,0)x's

SLEEVE

8(9¹/₂,10¹/₂)"
20.5(24,26.5)cm
48(58,64)rows

2" or 5cm
1x1rib

35(37,39)sts
7(7¹/₂,8)"
18(19,20.5)cm

1/2 COLLAR

k3rows
12rows
loop stitch

24(26,27)sts
6(6¹/₂,6³/₄)"
15(16,17)cm

CUFF

2" or 5cm
11rows loop st

28(30,32)sts
7(7¹/₂,8)"
18(19,20.5)cm

Tutti Frutti

For a festive unisex day suit, try this wide-striped QuickKnit™ number with its white ruffled collar. For boys, simply omit the collar and single-crochet around the neckline for a more tailored look.

■ Sizes

3–6 Months (12–18 Months, 2 Years)

Finished chest: 20 (22, 24) in./ 50 (54, 60) cm

■ Materials

DK cotton *that will obtain gauge below*

110 (155, 190) yd/100 (140, 173) m Green (A)

110 (155, 190) yd/100 (140, 173) m Red (B)

140 (200, 240) yd/128 (182, 219) m Blue (C)

55 yd/50 m White (D)

Straight needles, circular needles, and double-pointed needles (dpn) sizes 4, 6 US (10, 8 UK; 3.5, 4 mm), *or size needed to obtain gauge*

Four (5, 5) .75 in./2 cm buttons, stitch markers, and stitch holders

■ Gauge

20 sts and 28 rows = 4 in./10 cm in St st using larger needles

Always check gauge to save time and ensure correct yardage and correct fit! Always measure your child!

Sample in photographs knit in Rowan DK Cotton #241 Lettuce (A), #249 Pimpernel (B), #287 Diana (C), and #263 Bleached White (D).

■ Stripe Pattern

*2 in./5 cm each colors C, A, B; rep from *
(6 in./15 cm) for stripe pat.

■ Pant legs (make 2)

Cuff: With smaller needles and B, cast on 55
(59, 65) sts. Work in k1, p1 rib for 1 in./2.5
cm. Change to larger needles.

Leg: P next row on WS, inc 10 sts evenly
across, to 65 (69, 75) sts. Cont in St st and
stripe pat for 4 (6, 8) in./10 (15, 20) cm or
2 (3, 4) stripes above rib.

Crotch shaping: Beg RS, bind off 3 sts beg
next 2 rows. Dec 1 st each end every other
row twice, to 55 (59, 65) sts. With RS facing,
sl sts for one leg on larger circular needle,
and sl sts of other leg to same circular needle.
Cont to work back and forth in rows (beg and
end of row is center front) on 110 (118, 130)
sts until piece measures 6 (8, 10) in./15 (20,
25) cm or 3 (4, 5) stripes above rib.

■ Placket shaping

Bind off 3 sts at beg of next 2 rows to 104 (112, 124) sts. Cont in pat, dec 3 sts evenly across row every 1 in./2.5 cm twice, then dec 2 sts every 1 in./2.5 cm twice, to 94 (102, 114) sts. Work even until piece measures 9 (12.5, 14) in./23 (31.5, 35 cm) above rib.

■ Divide for front and back

On a RS row, work 22 (24, 27) sts for right front, place rem sts on a holder. Cont on these sts only until piece measures 12 (16, 18) in./30 (40, 45) cm or 6 (8, 9) stripes above rib.

Neck shaping: Bind off from neck edge 3 sts once, 2 sts 1 (2, 2) time, dec 1 st every other row 2 (1, 2) times. Work even until piece measures 14 (18, 20) in./35 (45, 50) cm or 7 (9, 10) stripes above rib. Place rem 15 (16, 18) sts on a holder for shoulder for later finishing.

■ Back

Sl next 50 (54, 60) sts to larger needle for back and work on these sts until same length as right front. Work 15 (16, 18) sts and place on a holder, bind off center 20 (22, 24) sts for neck, place rem 15 (16, 18) sts on a 2nd holder.

■ Left front

Sl rem 22 (24, 27) sts to larger needle and work to correspond to right front, reversing shaping.

Shoulder seams: *With wrong sides facing each other,* and larger dpn, place sts of back and front right shoulders on 2 parallel dpn. With a 3rd dpn and matching color, k through 1st st on each needle, then through the 2nd st on each needle, and pass 1st over 2nd to bind off. Cont in this way to end for a knitted seam. Work in same way for left shoulder seam.

■ Sleeves

Place markers on front and back 5 (5.5, 6) in./12.5 (14, 15) cm down from shoulder seams for armholes. With RS facing, larger dpn, and C, pick up and k 50 (56, 60) sts between markers. Join and work St st (k every rnd) and stripe pat, as foll: 4 rows even, then dec 1 st at beg and end of next rnd, then every 4th row 0 (2, 2) times more, then every other row 8 (9, 9) times, to 32 (32, 36) sts. Work even until 2 (3, 3) stripes have been worked, dec 0 (0, 4) sts evenly across last row, to 32 sts—piece measures approx 4 (6, 6) in./10 (15, 15) cm from pick-up row. Change to smaller dpn and C and work in k1, p1 rib for 1 in./2.5 cm. Bind off loosely and evenly in rib.

■ Finishing

Weave in all loose ends.

■ Collar

With RS facing, larger straight needles, and D, pick up and k 58 (62, 66) sts evenly around neck edge. Work in St st, inc 5 sts evenly across row every 3rd row for 2 in./5 cm. Inc 3 sts in each st on next row for ruffle. Work in k4, p4 rib for 3 rows. Bind off in rib.

■ Left front placket band

With RS facing, smaller straight needles, and A, pick up 36 (48, 48) sts evenly along left front placket band. Work in k1, p1 rib for 1 in./2.5 cm. Bind off in rib. Sew 4 (5, 5) but-

tons on band, the first one .75 in./2 cm from lower edge, the last .5 in./1.5 cm from top edge, and 2 (3, 3) others spaced evenly between.

■ Right front placket band

Work as for left front band, working button-holes opposite buttons in center of band by yo, k2tog for each buttonhole.

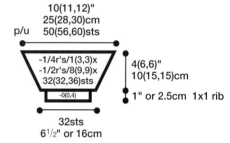

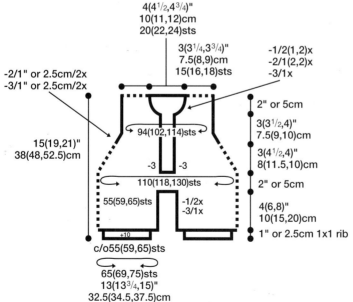

Jailbird

Jailbird is a romper—a wide-striped and unisex QuickKnit™, comfortable and festive. When my son was little, I decked him out in these tiny overalls constantly. Back then I could find these knitted rompers only in Europe, so I began to knit them up in batches—you will, too, when you find out how easy they are to make!

■ Sizes
3–6 Months (1, 2 Years)

Jumper finished chest: 20 (22, 23) in./51 (56, 58) cm

Hat finished circumference: 17 (17.5, 18) in./43 (44.5, 45.5) cm

■ Materials
100% mercerized cotton *that will obtain gauge below*

Jumper: 215 (280, 325) yd/195 (255, 295) m each White (A) and Green (B)

Hat: 100 (125, 150) yd/90 (114, 135) m each A and B; 5 yd/4.5 m Cerise (C) for topknot

Straight needles sizes 4, 6 US (10, 8 UK; 3.5, 4 mm), *or size needed to obtain gauge*

Circular needles sizes 4, 6 US (10, 8 UK; 3.5, 4 mm)

Double-pointed needles (dpn) size 6 US (8 UK, 4 mm)

Two .75 in./2 cm buttons, stitch holders, and stitch markers

■ Gauge
20 sts and 24 rows = 4 in./10 cm in St st using larger needles

Always check gauge to save time and ensure correct yardage and correct fit! Always measure your child!

■ Stripe Pattern
*6 rows (or 1 in./2.5 cm) each colors B, A; rep from * (12 rows or 2 in./5 cm) for stripe pat.

Sample in photograph knit in Rowan DK Cotton #263 White (A), #241 Lettuce (B), and #233 Cerise (C).

■ Pant legs (make 2)

Cuff: With smaller straight needles and A, cast on 55 (59, 63) sts. Work in k1, p1 rib for 1 in./2.5 cm. Change to larger straight needles. **Leg:** P next row on WS, inc 11 (12, 11) sts evenly across, to 66 (71, 74) sts. Cont in St st and stripe pat (beg with a B stripe), for 5 (6, 7) in./13 (15, 18) cm from beg, end with a full stripe.

Crotch shaping: Beg RS, bind off 3 sts beg next 2 rows. Dec 1 st each end every other row twice, to 56 (61, 64) sts. With RS facing, sl sts for one leg to larger circular needle, and sl sts of other leg to same circular needle. Join, place marker, and work in rnds on 112 (122, 128) sts in St st (k every rnd) and cont in stripe pat, until piece measures 7

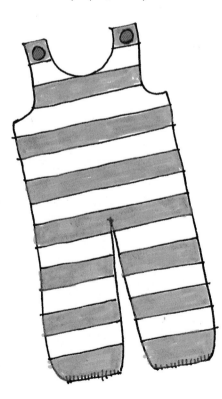

(9, 10) in./18 (23, 25.5) cm from beg. *Next rnd:* K26 (28, 30), [k2tog] twice, k52 (58, 60), [k2tog] twice, k to end of rnd. Work 4 rnds even. *Next rnd:* K25 (27, 29), [k2tog] twice, k50 (56, 58), [k2tog] twice, k to end. Work 4 rnds even. *Next rnd:* K24 (26, 28), [k2tog] twice, k48 (54, 56), [k2tog] twice, k to end. Work even on 100 (110, 116) sts until piece measures 11 (13, 14) in./28 (33, 35.5) cm from beg, end with a full stripe. **Divide for front and back:** Place 1st 25 (27, 29) sts and last 25 (28, 29) sts on a holder for the front.

■ Back

Cont to work back and forth on 50 (55, 58) back sts as foll:

Armhole: Bind off 2 sts at beg of next 2 rows, dec 1 st each side every other row twice. Work even on rem 42 (47, 50) sts until armhole measures 3 (4, 4) in./7.5 (10, 10) cm, end with a full stripe.

Neck shaping: Work 17 (18, 19) sts, join a 2nd skein of yarn and bind off center 8 (11, 12) sts, work to end. Working both sides at the same time with separate balls of yarn, bind off from each neck edge 3 sts once, 2 sts once, dec 1 st every other row twice. Work even on rem 10 (11, 12) sts until armhole measures 7 (8, 8) in./17.5 (20, 20) cm. Bind off.

■ Front

Work as for back until armhole measures 5.5 (6.5, 6.5) in./14 (16.5, 16.5) cm. Make a buttonhole (yo, k2tog) in center of each strap. Work even until armhole measures 6 (7, 7) in./15 (18, 18) cm. Work 3 rows next stripe, make 2nd buttonhole in center of each strap. Finish stripe, work 1 more contrasting stripe in garter st. Bind off.

■ Finishing

Weave in all loose ends. Sew crotch and leg seams. Sew buttons on back straps corresponding with buttonholes.

HAT

■ Rolled hem

With larger needles and A, cast on 75 (80, 83) sts. Work in St st for 10 rows. K next row, inc 10 (8, 8) sts evenly across, to 85 (88, 91) sts. P 1 row. Cont in St st and stripe pat as foll: *6 rows A, 6 rows B; rep from * once more. Cont with A only until piece measures 5 (5.75, 6.5) in./12.5 (14, 16.5) cm from beg, end with a WS row.

■ Top shaping

Next row (RS): *K2, k2tog; rep from *, end k1 (0, 3), to 64 (66, 69) sts. Work 1 row even. *Next row:* *K2, k2tog; rep from *, end k0 (2, 1), to 48 (50, 52) sts. Work 1 row even. *Next row:* *K2, k2tog; rep from *, end k0 (2, 0), to 36 (38, 39) sts. Work 1 row even. K2tog across next row, end k0 (0, 1), to 18 (19, 20) sts. P2tog across next row. K next row, dec to 6 sts. Place those 6 sts on dpn. With C, work I-cord on dpn as foll: K6, *slide sts to beg of needle to work next row from RS and k6; rep from * for 3.5 in./9 cm. Bind off. Tie I-cord in knot.

■ Finishing

Sew back seam, reversing seam on first 10 rows of St st for rolled edge. Weave in all loose ends.

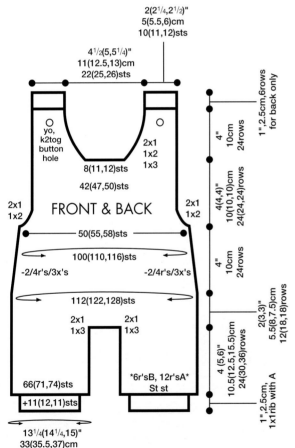

2(2¼,2½)"
5(5.5,6)cm
10(11,12)sts

4½(5,5¼)"
11(12.5,13)cm
22(25,26)sts

1",2.5cm,6rows
for back only

O
yo,
k2tog
button
hole

O

2x1
1x2
1x3

8(11,12)sts
42(47,50)sts

4"
10cm
24rows

4(4,4)"
10(10,10)cm
24(24,24)rows

2x1
1x2

FRONT & BACK

2x1
1x2

50(55,58)sts

100(110,116)sts

-2/4r's/3x's

-2/4r's/3x's

4"
10cm
24rows

112(122,128)sts

2x1
1x3

2x1
1x3

2(3,3)"
5.5(8,7.5)cm
12(18,18)rows

4 (5,6)"
10.5(12.5,15.5)cm
24(30,36)rows

66(71,74)sts

6r'sB, 12r'sA
St st

+11(12,11)sts

1",2.5cm,
1x1 rib with A

13¼(14¼,15)"
33(35.5,37)cm
c/o55 (59,63)sts

Denim Bibs

Cotton denim QuickKnit™ bib overalls with a front zipper and shoulder buttons make for easy dressing and comfortable play. Knit in real denim yarn, they will wash, wear, and shrink just like your favorite jeans. If you are using another regular yarn, please remember to read the pattern carefully and adjust accordingly.

■ Sizes

3–6 Months (1, 2, 3 Years)

Finished waist: 20 (22, 23, 24) in./51 (56, 58.5, 61) cm

■ Materials

DK cotton denim yarn *that will obtain gauge below*

310 (440, 610, 695) yd/282 (401, 556, 633) m (*Note:* This yarn shrinks by 20 percent in length. Extra length has been added to accommodate this shrinkage. For other denim yarns, make legs 1 in./2.5 cm shorter.)

Straight needles and circular needles size 6 US (8 UK, 4 mm), *or size needed to obtain gauge*

Two .75 in./2 cm buttons, a 5 (5, 7, 7) in./12.5 (12.5, 18, 18) cm zipper, and stitch holders

Sample in photographs knit in Rowan Den-M-Nit 100% cotton #225 Nashville.

■ Gauge

20 sts and 24 rows = 4 in./10 cm in St st using size 6 needles

Always check gauge to save time and ensure correct yardage and correct fit! Always measure your child!

■ Pant legs (make two)

Cuff: Cast on 42 (50, 60, 64) sts. Work 4 rows in garter st (k every row).

Leg: Cont in St st, inc 1 st each side every 4th row 5 (6, 9, 9) times, every 2nd row 4 (3, 0, 0) times, to 60 (68, 78, 82) sts. Work even until piece measures 5.5 (6, 6.5, 7) in./14 (15.5, 16.5, 17.5) cm from beg.

Crotch shaping: Beg RS, bind off 3 sts beg next 2 rows. Dec 1 st each end every other row twice, to 50 (58, 68, 72) sts. With RS facing, sl sts for one leg onto circular needle, and sl sts of other leg to same circular needle. Cont to work back and forth in rows (beg and end of row is center front), and work first and last st in garter st for selvage, on 100 (116, 136, 144) sts until piece measures 10.5 (15, 14, 14.5) in./26.5 (38, 35.5, 36.5) cm from beg, end with a WS row. **1, 2, and 3 Years only:** *Next row (RS):* K (27, 32, 34), [k2tog] twice, k to last (31, 36, 38) sts, [k2tog] twice, k (27, 32, 34). Work 3 rows even. *Next row (RS):* Work (26, 31, 33), [k2tog] twice, k to last (30, 35, 37) sts, [k2tog] twice, k (26, 31, 33). Cont in this way to dec 4 sts every 4th row (0, 3, 4) times more. **All sizes:** Work even on 100 (108, 116, 120) sts until piece measures 10.5 (16, 17, 18) in./26.5 (40.5, 43, 45.5) cm from beg.

Divide for front and back: Place first 25 (27, 29, 30) sts and last 25 (27, 29, 30) sts on a holder for front. Cont on 50 (54, 58, 60) back sts.

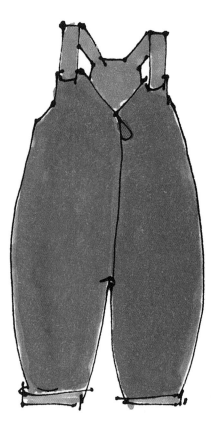

Armhole shaping: *Next row (RS):* K3, k2tog, work to last 5 sts, k2tog, k3. *Next row:* K3, p to last 3 sts, k3. Cont to work 3 sts each side in garter st and dec 1 st each side (inside of garter st) every 2nd row 2 (1, 2, 1) times, every 4th row 6 (8, 8, 9) times, to 32 (34, 36, 38) sts, AT THE SAME TIME, after the 4th (6th, 6th, 7th) dec, work garter st on all sts. After all armhole decs, bind off center 18 (20, 20, 22) sts for neck and, working both sides at same time, work in garter st on rem 7 (7, 8, 8) sts each side for strap for 4 (4.5, 5, 5.5) in./10 (11.5, 12.5, 14) cm, or 1 in./2.5 cm less than desired length. Work a buttonhole on each strap as foll: K3, yo, k2tog, k2 (2, 3, 3). Work 1 in./2.5 cm more. Bind off.

■ Right front

Sl first 25 (27, 29, 30) sts from holder to needle for right front. Work armhole shaping at end of RS rows as for back, AT THE SAME TIME, after 1.5 (2.25, 2.5, 2.5) in./4 (5.5, 6.5, 6.5) cm of shaping has been worked, work 3 sts at neck edge in garter st and dec 1 st at neck edge at beg of RS rows (inside of garter

st) every other row 9 (10, 10, 11) times. After all decs, bind off rem 7 (7, 8, 8) sts.

■ Left front

Work to correspond to right front, reversing shaping.

■ Finishing

Sew zipper in center of fronts, inside garter st selvage, so that the top of the zipper ends at the V-shaping. Sew rem crotch and leg seams. Sew buttons on front.

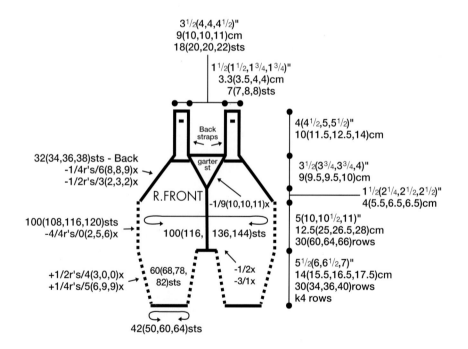

Parka

A completely reversible mohair jacket, with tweed I-cord trim and reversible ties, this parka jacket is light but toasty warm, buffering against the winter chill. Europeans knit in mohair for their kids all the time; do they know something we don't? Two jackets in one give you plenty of color options.

■ **Sizes**

2 (4, 6) Years

Finished chest (closed): 29 (32, 34) in./72 (80, 86) cm

Length, shoulder to hem: 13 (16, 17.5) in./32.5 (40.5, 44) cm

■ **Materials**

Worsted weight mohair and wool *that will obtain gauge below*

480 (630, 735) yd/440 (575, 670) m each Red (A) and Green (B)

20 yd/19 m Black/White Marl (C) (*Note:* Parka is made in two pieces of identical size in different colors, which are sewn tog for double thickness, reversible look.)

Straight needles and double-pointed needles (dpn) sizes 5, 6 US (9, 8 UK; 3.75, 4 mm), *or size needed to obtain gauge*

Stitch holders and stitch markers

■ **Gauge**

20 sts and 28 rows = 4 in./10 cm in St st using larger needles

Always check gauge to save time and ensure correct yardage and correct fit! Always measure your child!

Sample in photograph knit in Rowan Kid Silk #985 Pillar (A), #974 Apple (B), and Rowan Lightweight DK Marl Wool #825 Licorice (C).

■ Body

With larger needles and A, cast on 144 (160, 172) sts. Work in St st (k on RS, p on WS) for 6 (8.5, 9.5) in./15 (21.5, 24) cm, end with a WS row.

Divide for front and back: *Next row (RS):* Work 36 (40, 43) sts for right front and place on a holder, work 72 (80, 86) sts for back, place rem 36 (40, 43) sts on a 2nd holder for left front. Cont on back sts only until piece measures 13 (16, 17.5) in./32.5 (40.5, 44) cm from beg. Work 24 (27, 29) sts for one shoulder and place on a 3rd holder, bind off 24 (26, 28) sts for back neck, work rem sts for 2nd shoulder and place on a 4th holder.

■ Right front

Sl sts from right front holder to needle and cont on these sts until piece measures 11.5 (14.5, 16) in./28.5 (36.5, 40) cm from beg, end with a WS row.

Neck shaping: *Next row (RS):* Bind off 4 (5, 6) sts (neck edge), work to end. Cont to bind off from neck edge 3 sts twice, 2 sts once. When same length as back, place rem 24 (27, 29) sts on a 5th holder for shoulder.

■ Left front

Work to correspond to right front, reversing neck shaping.

Shoulder seams: *With wrong sides facing each other* and larger dpn, place sts of back

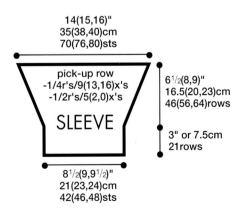

and front right shoulders on 2 parallel dpn. With a 3rd dpn and A, k through 1st st on each needle, then through the 2nd st on each needle, and pass 1st over 2nd to bind off. Cont in this way to end for a knitted seam. Work in same way for left shoulder seam.

■ Sleeves

With RS facing, larger dpn, and A, pick up and k 70 (76, 80) sts around armhole edge. Join and place marker at underarm. Work in St st (k every rnd), dec 1 st each end (k2tog

14(15,16)"
35(38,40)cm
70(76,80)sts

pick-up row
-1/4r's/9(13,16)x's
-1/2r's/5(2,0)x's

SLEEVE

6¹/₂(8,9)"
16.5(20,23)cm
46(56,64)rows

3" or 7.5cm
21rows

8¹/₂(9,9¹/₂)"
21(23,24)cm
42(46,48)sts

before and after marker), every 4th rnd 9 (13, 16) times, every 2nd rnd 5 (2, 0) times, to 42 (46, 48) sts. Work even until sleeve measures 9.5 (11, 12) in./24 (27.5, 30.5) cm. Bind off loosely.

■ Finishing

Collar: With RS facing, smaller needles, and A, beg at right front neck, pick up and k 71 (75, 79) sts evenly around neck edge. *Next row (WS):* P3, *k1, p3; rep from * to end. *Next row:* K the k sts and p the p sts. Rep last row for 1.25 in./3 cm. Bind off in rib.

■ Reverse

Make a 2nd garment in same way but with color B. Join both garments as foll: With RS of each garment facing each other, insert garment B inside garment A. With WS of garment A facing, sewing through both thicknesses, sew lower edge of sleeves tog. Work

in same way around entire outside edge of parka, leaving 4 in./10 cm unsewn at lower edge of each front. Turn parka inside out to right side and complete seam.

■ I-cord edging

With smaller dpn and C, cast on 4 sts. K4, *slide sts to beg of needle and k4; rep from * until cord fits around entire outside edge of parka. Do not bind off. Sew edging around parka, adjusting length if necessary. Bind off. Sew ends of cord tog.

■ I-cord toggles (make 6)

Work as for edging for 6 in./15.5 cm. Bind off. Weave toggles through both thicknesses on each front, the 1st pair at 7 in./18 cm from lower edge, the 2nd pair just below collar, and the 3rd pair evenly between. Tie a knot at each end of toggle to secure.

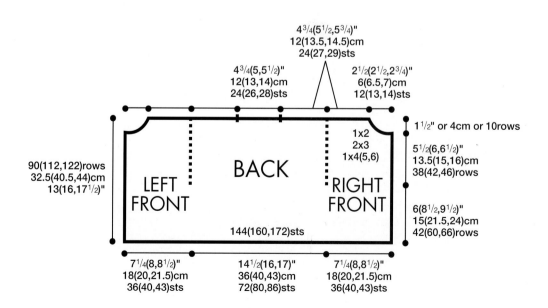

4³/₄(5¹/₂,5³/₄)"
12(13.5,14.5)cm
24(27,29)sts

4³/₄(5,5¹/₂)"
12(13,14)cm
24(26,28)sts

2¹/₂(2¹/₂,2³/₄)"
6(6.5,7)cm
12(13,14)sts

90(112,122)rows
32.5(40.5,44)cm
13(16,17¹/₂)"

LEFT FRONT

BACK

RIGHT FRONT

1x2
2x3
1x4(5,6)

1¹/₂" or 4cm or 10rows

5¹/₂(6,6¹/₂)"
13.5(15,16)cm
38(42,46)rows

6(8¹/₂,9¹/₂)"
15(21.5,24)cm
42(60,66)rows

144(160,172)sts

7¹/₄(8,8¹/₂)"
18(20,21.5)cm
36(40,43)sts

14¹/₂(16,17)"
36(40,43)cm
72(80,86)sts

7¹/₄(8,8¹/₂)"
18(20,21.5)cm
36(40,43)sts

Popcorn

Baby's bunting is a QuickKnit™ in bulky cotton chenille, with comfortable leggings to fit in the car seat or baby carrier, and removable mitten hand coverings. Sprinkled with crocheted popcorn bobbles, this contemporary bunting makes a bold design statement.

■ Sizes

Newborn (6, 12 Months)

Finished chest: 28 (32, 34) in./71 (81, 86) cm

Length, shoulder to foot: 22 (23.5, 25) in./56 (59.5, 63.5) cm

■ Materials

Bulky weight chenille *that will obtain gauge below*

770 (850, 925) yd/700 (770, 840) m Black (MC)

10 yd/10 m White (CC) (*Note:* Bobbles are crocheted with CC and applied as desired after pieces are knit.)

Straight needles and double-pointed needles (dpn) size 8 US (6 UK, 5 mm), *or size needed to obtain gauge*

Crochet hook size F (8 UK, 4 mm)

One red zipper 14 in./36 cm long, stitch markers, and stitch holders

■ Gauge

14 sts and 22 rows = 4 in./10 cm in St st using size 8 needles

Always check gauge to save time and ensure correct yardage and correct fit! Always measure your child!

Sample in photographs knit in Rowan Chunky Chenille in #367 Black (MC) and #365 Ecru (CC).

■ Back

Right leg: With MC, cast on 11 (14, 16) sts. Work in garter st (k every row), inc 1 st each side every other row 6 times, to 23 (26, 28) sts. Work even in garter st until piece measures 3 in./7.5 cm from beg. Cont in St st until piece measures 5.5 (7, 8.5) in./14 (17.5, 21.5) cm from beg, ending with a WS row. Place sts on a holder.

Left leg: Work as for right leg.

Join legs: *Next row (RS):* Work 23 (26, 28) sts of right leg, cast on 4 sts (crotch), work across 23 (26, 28) sts of left leg, to 50 (56, 60) sts. Work even until piece measures 15.75 in./40 cm from crotch.

Neck shaping: *Next row (RS):* Work 19 (22, 23) sts, join a 2nd skein and bind off center 12 (12, 14) sts, work to end. Working both sides at same time, bind off 2 sts from each neck edge twice. Place rem 15 (18, 19) sts each side on a holder for shoulders for later finishing.

■ Front

Work same as back through leg joining. K 2 rows on 50 (56, 60) sts.

Separate for zipper: *Next row (RS):* K 25 (28, 30) sts, join a 2nd skein of MC, k to end. *Next row (WS):* P23 (26, 28), k2 (garter trim); on 2nd half, k2 (garter trim), p23 (26, 28). Cont in this way until zipper opening measures 14 in./35.5 cm.

Neck shaping: Bind off from each neck edge 5 (5, 6) sts once, 2 sts once, and 1 st 3 times. When same length as back, place on holders rem 15 (18, 19) sts each side for shoulders.

■ Sleeves

Mitten: With MC, cast on 10 (14, 16) sts. K 1 row. Working in garter st, cast on 2 sts beg of next 10 rows, to 30 (34, 36) sts. Work even in garter st until piece measures 3 in./7.5 cm from beg. Place sts on a holder.

■ Lining

Separately, cast on 20 sts. Work in St st for 1.5 in./4 cm. Bind off 5 sts at beg of next 2 rows, 10 lining sts rem. Return to mitten sts and k 10 (12, 13), bind off center 10 sts, k 10 (12, 13). On next WS row, p to bound-off sts, p 10 lining sts, p to end. Cont in St st, inc 1 st each side every 4th row 1 (4, 5) times, every other row 3 (0, 0) times, to 38 (42, 46) sts. Work even until piece measures 5.5 (6.5, 8) in./14 (16.5, 20) cm from beg. Bind off.

Shoulder seam: *With wrong sides facing each other,* place sts of back and front right shoul-

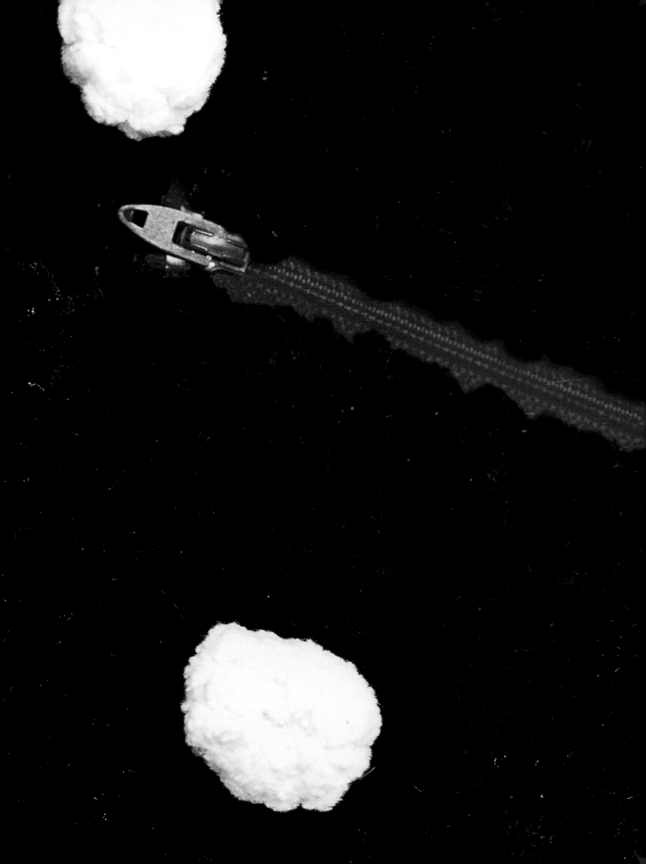

ders on 2 parallel dpn. With a 3rd dpn, k through 1st st on each needle, then through the 2nd st on each needle, and pass 1st over 2nd to bind off. Cont in this way to end for a knitted seam. Sew left shoulder seam in same way. **Finishing:** With WS facing each other, place sts of back and front right shoulders on 2 parallel dpn. With a 3rd dpn, k through 1st st on each needle, then through 2nd st on each needle; pass 1st over 2nd to bind off. Cont in this way to end for a knitted seam. Sew left shoulder seam in same way. Place markers 5.5 (6, 6.5) in./14 (15, 16.5) cm down from shoulder seams on front and back for armholes. Sew 5 bound-off sts and sides of lining to WS of mitten, leaving cast-on edge free. Sew sleeves to armholes between markers. Sew side, leg, and crotch seams. Sew sleeve seams. Sew in zipper.

■ Hood

Pick up 27 (27, 29) sts around right front neck to center back neck. Keeping center front 2 sts in garter st, work in St st for 5.5 (6, 7) in./14 (15, 17.5) cm.

Top shaping: *Next row (WS):* Bind off 3 sts (center edge), work to end. Cont to bind off 3 sts from center edge twice more, then 2 sts 4 times. Bind off rem 10 (10, 12) sts. Beg at center back neck with MC, pick up and k sts around to center left neck and work other half of hood to correspond, reversing shaping. With RS facing each other, sew hood seam.

■ Bobbles (make 15 or as desired)

With CC, make a lp on hook, ch 1, 6 sc in lp. *Rnd 2:* 2 sc in each sc. *Rnd 3:* Dec 1 sc in each sc. Pull through lps tightly, and pull both ends to lower part of bobble. Sew on bobbles.

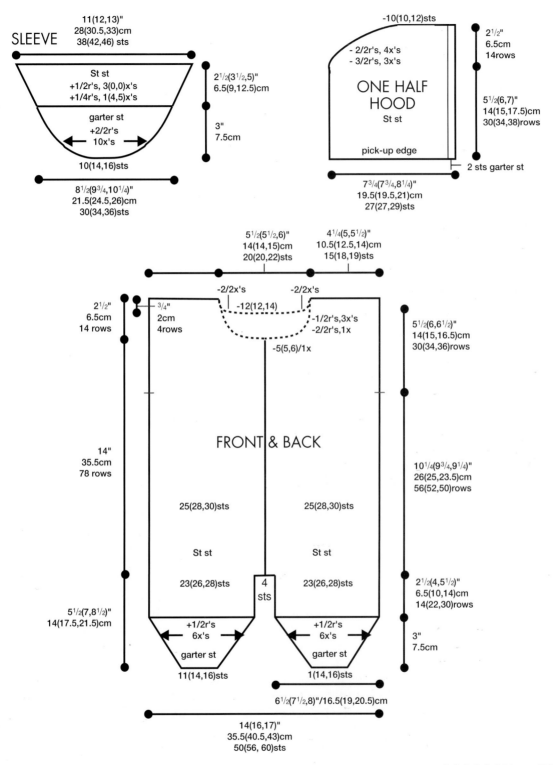

SLEEVE

11(12,13)"
28(30.5,33)cm
38(42,46) sts

St st
+1/2r's, 3(0,0)x's
+1/4r's, 1(4,5)x's

garter st
+2/2r's
10x's

2¹/₂(3¹/₂,5)"
6.5(9,12.5)cm

3"
7.5cm

10(14,16)sts

8¹/₂(9³/₄,10¹/₄)"
21.5(24.5,26)cm
30(34,36)sts

-10(10,12)sts

- 2/2r's, 4x's
- 3/2r's, 3x's

ONE HALF
HOOD
St st

pick-up edge

2¹/₂"
6.5cm
14rows

5¹/₂(6,7)"
14(15,17.5)cm
30(34,38)rows

2 sts garter st

7³/₄(7³/₄,8¹/₄)"
19.5(19.5,21)cm
27(27,29)sts

5¹/₂(5¹/₂,6)"
14(14,15)cm
20(20,22)sts

4¹/₄(5,5¹/₂)"
10.5(12.5,14)cm
15(18,19)sts

-2/2x's   -2/2x's
-12(12,14)

-1/2r's,3x's
-2/2r's,1x

-5(5,6)/1x

2¹/₂"
6.5cm
14 rows

³/₄"
2cm
4rows

5¹/₂(6,6¹/₂)"
14(15,16.5)cm
30(34,36)rows

14"
35.5cm
78 rows

FRONT & BACK

25(28,30)sts   25(28,30)sts

St st   St st

23(26,28)sts   4   23(26,28)sts
                sts

+1/2r's   +1/2r's
6x's   6x's
garter st   garter st

11(14,16)sts   1(14,16)sts

10¹/₄(9³/₄,9¹/₄)"
26(25,23.5)cm
56(52,50)rows

2¹/₂(4,5¹/₂)"
6.5(10,14)cm
14(22,30)rows

3"
7.5cm

5¹/₂(7,8¹/₂)"
14(17.5,21.5)cm

6¹/₂(7¹/₂,8)"/16.5(19,20.5)cm

14(16,17)"
35.5(40.5,43)cm
50(56, 60)sts

Snowflake

Fair Isle knitting can be challenging, but this tunic in wool with an overall snowflake pattern and contrasting ribbing and trim is done with only two colors at a time. The long sweater is warm, and the colorways are both pretty and unusual.

■ Sizes

2 (4, 6, 8) Years

Finished chest: 27 (30, 32, 35) in./68 (76, 80, 88) cm

Length, shoulder to hem: 17 (20, 21.5, 24) in./43 (50.5, 54, 61) cm

■ Materials

DK weight wool *that will obtain gauge below*

570 (735, 850, 1015) yd/520 (670, 775, 925) m in Green (MC)

350 (450, 520, 615) yd/320 (410, 470, 560) m in Blue (A)

45 (55, 60, 70) yd/40 (50, 55, 65) m in Yellow (B)

15 yd/14 m in Red (C)

Straight needles and double-pointed needles (dpn) size 5 US (9 UK, 3.75 mm), *or size needed to obtain gauge*

Circular needle size 5 US (9 UK, 3.75 mm), 16 in./40 cm long

Stitch holders and stitch markers

■ Gauge

26 sts and 26 rows = 4 in./10 cm in St st and chart pat using size 5 needles

Always check gauge to save time and ensure correct yardage and correct fit! Always measure your child!

Sample in photographs knit in Rowan DK Wool #124 (MC), #56 (A), #12 (B), and #42 (C).

■ Corrugated Rib (multiple of 4 sts plus 2)

Preparation row (RS): *K2 A, k2 B; rep from *, end k2 A.

Row 1 (WS): *P2 A, k2 B; rep from *, end p2 A.

Row 2: K the k sts with A and p the p sts with B.

Rep rows 1 and 2 for corrugated rib.

■ Back

With straight needles and C, cast on 94 (106, 144, 122) sts. Work in corrugated rib for 1.5 in./4 cm, end with a RS row. With MC, p next row on WS, dec 7 (9, 9, 9) sts evenly across, to 87 (97, 105, 113) sts.

Beg chart pat: *Next row (RS):* Beg with st 13 (16, 12, 16), work to end of chart, work 16-st rep 5 (6, 6, 7) times, work st 1 to 3 (0, 4, 0) once more. Cont in chart pat as est, working rows 1–18 once, then cont to rep rows 5–18 until piece measures 17 (20, 21.5, 24)

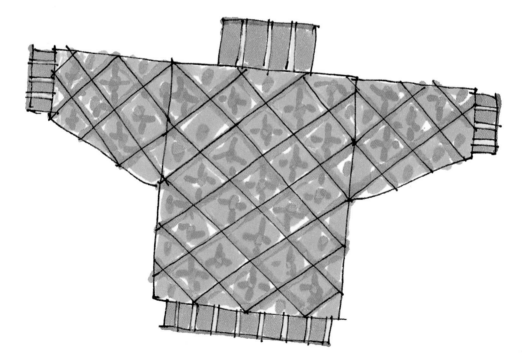

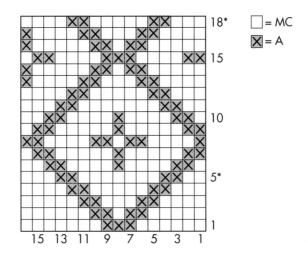

☐ = MC
☒ = A

in./43 (50.5, 54, 61) cm from beg. Place 26 (29, 31, 35) sts on a holder for one shoulder, place next 35 (39, 43, 43) sts on a 2nd holder for back neck, place rem 26 (29, 31, 35) sts on a 3rd holder for other shoulder.

■ Front

Work as for back until piece measures 14.5 (17.5, 19, 21.5) in./36.5 (44, 47.5, 54.5) cm from beg, end with a WS row.

Neck shaping: *Next row (RS):* Work 32 (35, 37, 41) sts, join a 2nd skein of yarn and bind off center 23 (27, 31, 31) sts, work to end. Working both sides at same time, bind off from each neck edge 2 sts twice, 1 st twice. Work even until same length as back. Place rem 26 (29, 31, 35) sts each side on holders for later finishing.

Shoulder seams: *With wrong sides facing each other,* place sts of back and front right shoulders on 2 parallel dpn. With a 3rd dpn and MC, k through 1st st on each needle, then through the 2nd st on each needle, and pass 1st over 2nd to bind off. Cont in this way to end for a knitted seam. Work in same way for left shoulder seam.

■ Sleeves

Place markers on front and back 6 (6.5, 7, 7.5) in./15 (16.5, 17.5, 19) cm down from shoulder seams for armholes. With RS facing and MC, pick up and k 79 (85, 91, 97) sts between markers. Work in St st and chart pat as foll: Beg with st 9 (14, 11, 16), work to end of chart, work 16-st rep 4 (5, 5, 6) times, work st 1 to 7 (2, 5, 0) once more. Cont in chart pat as est and work decs as foll: Dec 1 st each end every 4th row 7 (10, 10, 11) times, every other row 11 (10, 13,

13) times, to 43 (45, 45, 49) sts. Cont in pat until sleeve measures 8.5 (10, 11, 11.75) in./21.5 (25, 28, 29.5) cm, end with a WS row. With MC, p next row on WS, dec 5 (3, 3, 3) sts evenly across, to 38 (42, 42, 46) sts. Work 1.5 in./4 cm in corrugated rib. With C, bind off loosely and evenly knitwise.

■ Finishing

For neckband, with RS facing, circular needle, and A, pick up and k 100 (108, 116, 116) sts evenly around neck. Join and work in corrugated rib for 1.75 in./4.5 cm. With C, bind off loosely and evenly knitwise. Sew side and sleeve seams.

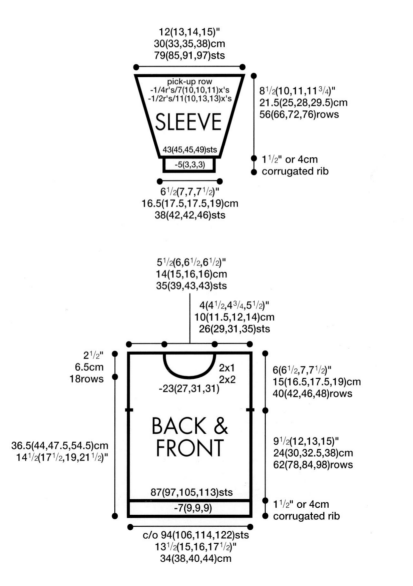

12(13,14,15)"
30(33,35,38)cm
79(85,91,97)sts

pick-up row
-1/4r's/7(10,10,11)x's
-1/2r's/11(10,13,13)x's

SLEEVE

8¹/2(10,11,11³/4)"
21.5(25,28,29.5)cm
56(66,72,76)rows

43(45,45,49)sts
-5(3,3,3)

1¹/2" or 4cm
corrugated rib

6¹/2(7,7,7¹/2)"
16.5(17.5,17.5,19)cm
38(42,42,46)sts

5¹/2(6,6¹/2,6¹/2)"
14(15,16,16)cm
35(39,43,43)sts

4(4¹/2,4³/4,5¹/2)"
10(11.5,12,14)cm
26(29,31,35)sts

2¹/2"
6.5cm
18rows

2x1
2x2
-23(27,31,31)

6(6¹/2,7,7¹/2)"
15(16.5,17.5,19)cm
40(42,46,48)rows

BACK &
FRONT

36.5(44,47.5,54.5)cm
14¹/2(17¹/2,19,21¹/2)"

9¹/2(12,13,15)"
24(30,32.5,38)cm
62(78,84,98)rows

87(97,105,113)sts
-7(9,9,9)

1¹/2" or 4cm
corrugated rib

c/o 94(106,114,122)sts
13¹/2(15,16,17¹/2)"
34(38,40,44)cm

Aran Pull

Sized from two to ten, this QuickKnit™ cabled pullover couldn't be simpler, while looking complicated and accomplished. The bulky yarn makes it possible to work up even the larger sizes before the kids go to college!

■ Sizes

2 (4, 6, 8, 10) Years

Finished chest: 25 (28, 30, 32, 34) in./63 (71, 76, 81, 86) cm

Length, shoulder to hem: 13 (16, 17.5, 19, 20.5) in./33 (40.5, 44.5, 48.5, 52) cm

■ Materials

Bulky weight wool *that will obtain gauge below*

500 (660, 800, 900, 1050) yd/450 (590, 720, 810, 945) m Natural

Needles sizes 8, 10 US (6, 4 UK; 5, 6 mm), *or size needed to obtain gauge*

Circular needle size 8 US (6 UK, 5 mm), 16 in./40 cm long

Double-pointed needles (dpn) size 10 US (4 UK, 6 mm)

Cable needle (cn)

Stitch holders and stitch markers

■ Gauge

14 sts and 22 rows = 4 in./10 cm in seed st using larger needles

19 sts cable panel = 3.25 in./8 cm using larger needles

Always check gauge to save time and ensure correct yardage and correct fit! Always measure your child!

Sample in studio photograph knit in Rowan Chunky Wool #810 Snowberry; sample in location photograph (page 163) knit in Cynthia Helene Bulky Merino, Natural.

■ Seed Stitch

Row 1: *K1, p1; rep from *.

Row 2: K the p sts and p the k sts.

Rep row 2 for seed st.

■ Left Twist—LT (over 2 sts)

Row 1 (RS): K 2nd st on LH needle behind 1st st, then k 1st st, drop both sts from needle.

Row 2: P2.

Rep rows 1 and 2 for LT.

■ 4-St (6-St) Cable

Rows 1 and 3 (RS): K4 (6).

Row 2 and all WS rows: P4 (6).

Row 5: Sl 2 sts to cn and hold to *back* of work, k2, k2 from cn (sl 3 sts to cn and hold to *back* of work, k3, k3 from cn).

Row 7: Rep row 1.

Row 8: Rep row 2.

Rep rows 1–8 for 4-st (6-st) cable.

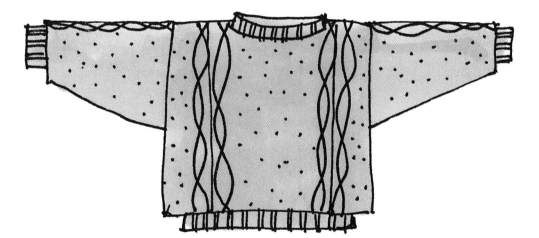

■ Back

With smaller needles, cast on 45 (51, 55, 57, 61) sts. Work in k1, p1 rib for 1 (1, 1.5, 1.5, 1.5) in./2.5 (2.5, 4, 4, 4) cm, inc 14 (15, 15, 16, 16) sts evenly across last WS row, to 59 (66, 70, 73, 77) sts. Change to larger needles. **Beg cable pat:** *Next row (RS):* Work 3 (4, 6, 7, 8) sts in seed st, *p1, LT over 2 sts, p1*, 4-st cable, rep between *s, 6-st cable, p1, 15 (20, 20, 21, 23) sts seed st, p1, 6-st cable, rep between *s, 4-st cable, rep between *s, 3 (4, 6, 7, 8) sts in seed st. Cont in pats as est until piece measures 13 (16, 17.5, 19, 20.5) in./33 (40.5, 44.5, 48.5, 52) cm from beg. Place 20 (23, 24, 25, 26) sts on a holder for one shoulder,

place next 19 (20, 22, 23, 25) sts on a 2nd holder for back neck, place rem 20 (23, 24, 25, 26) sts on a 3rd holder for other shoulder.

■ Front

Work as for back until piece measures 11 (13.5, 15, 16.5, 18) in./28 (34, 38, 42, 46) cm from beg.

Neck shaping: Work as foll: *Next row (RS):* Work 26 (29, 31, 32, 33) sts, join a 2nd skein of yarn and bind off center 7 (8, 8, 9, 11) sts, work to end. Working both sides at

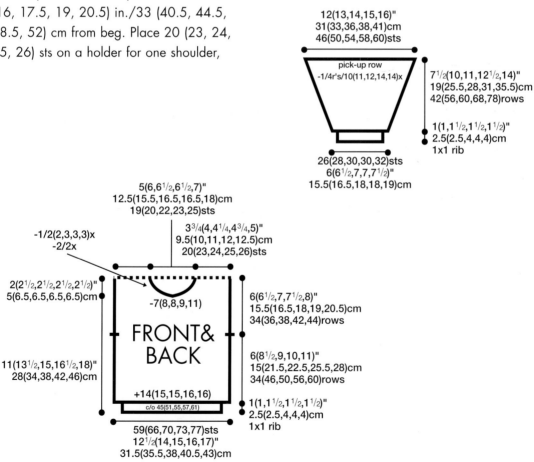

12(13,14,15,16)"
31(33,36,38,41)cm
46(50,54,58,60)sts

pick-up row
-1/4r's/10(11,12,14,14)x

7¹/₂(10,11,12¹/₂,14)"
19(25.5,28,31,35.5)cm
42(56,60,68,78)rows

1(1,1¹/₂,1¹/₂,1¹/₂)"
2.5(2.5,4,4,4)cm
1x1 rib

26(28,30,30,32)sts
6(6¹/₂,7,7,7¹/₂)"
15.5(16.5,18,18,19)cm

5(6,6¹/₂,6¹/₂,7)"
12.5(15.5,16.5,16.5,18)cm
19(20,22,23,25)sts

-1/2(2,3,3,3)x
-2/2x

3³/₄(4,4¹/₄,4³/₄,5)"
9.5(10,11,12,12.5)cm
20(23,24,25,26)sts

2(2¹/₂,2¹/₂,2¹/₂,2¹/₂)"
5(6.5,6.5,6.5,6.5)cm

-7(8,8,9,11)

FRONT&
BACK

6(6¹/₂,7,7¹/₂,8)"
15.5(16.5,18,19,20.5)cm
34(36,38,42,44)rows

11(13¹/₂,15,16¹/₂,18)"
28(34,38,42,46)cm

6(8¹/₂,9,10,11)"
15(21.5,22.5,25.5,28)cm
34(46,50,56,60)rows

+14(15,15,16,16)
c/o 45(51,55,57,61)

1(1,1¹/₂,1¹/₂,1¹/₂)"
2.5(2.5,4,4,4)cm
1x1 rib

59(66,70,73,77)sts
12¹/₂(14,15,16,17)"
31.5(35.5,38,40.5,43)cm

same time, bind off from each neck edge 2 sts twice, 1 st 2 (2, 3, 3, 3) times. Work even until same length as back. Place rem 20 (23, 24, 25, 26) sts each side on holders for later finishing.

Shoulder seams: *With wrong sides facing each other*, place sts of back and front right shoulders on 2 parallel dpn. With a 3rd dpn and MC, k through 1st st on each needle, then through the 2nd st on each needle, and pass 1st over 2nd to bind off. Cont in this way to end for a knitted seam. Work in same way for left shoulder seam.

■ Sleeves

Place markers on front and back 6 (6.5, 7, 7.5, 8) in./15.5 (16.5, 18, 19, 20.5) cm down from shoulder seams for armholes. With RS facing, pick up and k 46 (50, 54, 58, 60) sts between markers. **Est cable pat:** *Next row (WS):* Work 17 (19, 21, 23, 24) sts in seed st, k1, p2 (row 2 of LT), k1, p2 (row 2 of 4-st cable), k1, p2 (row 2 of LT), k1,17 (19, 21, 23, 24) sts in seed st. Cont in pats as est for 4 rows more, then dec 1 st each end of next row, then every 4th row 9 (10, 11, 13, 13) times more. When sleeve measures 7.5 (10, 11, 12.5, 14) in./19 (25.5, 28, 32, 35.5) cm, work 1 (1, 1.5, 1.5, 1.5) in./2.5 (2.5, 4, 4, 4) cm in k1, p1 rib on rem 26 (28, 30, 30, 32) sts. Bind off loosely and evenly in rib.

■ Finishing

For neckband, with circular needle, k 19 (20, 22, 23, 25) sts from back neck holder, pick up and k 41 (42, 44, 45, 47) sts along front neck. Join and work in k1, p1 rib on 60 (62, 66, 68, 72) sts for 1 in./2.5 cm. Bind off loosely and evenly in rib. Sew side and sleeve seams.

Twizzle Tops

Color-blocked with ridges and a flat top with an I-cord topknot, this cap is knit on four needles from the top down in wool. The yarn you purchase will be enough for two hats, but two hats may not be enough to fill all your orders! I've found that teenagers and cross-country skiers love this cap, too.

■ Sizes

Newborn (Small, Medium, Large)

Circumference: 16 (18, 20, 22) in./41 (48, 53, 56) cm

■ Materials

DK wool *that will obtain gauge below*

50 yd/45 m each:

Colorway 1: Purple (A), Light Green (B), Red (C), Turquoise (D), Yellow (E), Blue (F)

Colorway 2: Red (A), Purple (B), Turquoise (C), Yellow (D), Blue (E), Light Green (F)

One set (5) double-pointed needles (dpn) size 6 US (8 UK, 4 mm), *or size needed to obtain gauge*

■ Gauge

24 sts and 32 rows = 4 in./10 cm in St st using size 6 needles

Always check gauge to save time and ensure correct yardage and correct fit! Always measure your child!

Samples in photograph knit in Rowan DK Wool #501 Purple (Colorway 1: A), #32 Light Green (B), #115 Red (C), #90 Turquoise (D), #13 Yellow (E), and #51 Blue (F).

■ Twizzle top

With 2 dpn and A, cast on 4 sts. Work I-cord as foll: *Row 1 (RS):* K4. *Do not turn work. Slide sts to other end of needle to work next row from RS, and k4; rep from * for 3 in./7.5 cm.

■ Hat body

Inc 1 st in each st on next row, to 8 sts. Divide sts evenly over 4 dpn (2 sts on each needle). Change to B. Join and work in rnds of St st (k every rnd), inc 1 st at end of every needle every rnd (therefore 4 sts inc'd every rnd) until there are 96 (108, 120, 132) sts, or 24 (27, 30, 33) sts on each needle. Change to C and k 1 rnd, p 4 rnds. Change to D and k 2 rnds. *Next rnd:* *K5 D, k1 E (colorway 1) or k1 A (colorway 2); rep from * around. With D, k 4 rnds. *Next rnd:* *K2 D, k1 E or A, k3 D; rep from * around. With D, k 2 rnds. With A (colorway 1) or E (colorway 2), k 1 rnd, p 4 rnds. With F, k 2 rnds. Next 3 rnds *k2 F, k1 B (colorway 1) or k1 A (colorway 2); rep from * around. With F, k 2 rnds.

■ I-cord border

With 2 dpn and C, cast on 4 sts and work I-cord as for top, attaching cord to lower edge of hat by knitting last st of I-cord tog with 1 st from hat. Cont in this way until all sts are worked on hat, then bind off rem I-cord sts. Sew bound-off and cast-on sts of I-cord tog. Weave in all loose ends. Tie top-knot.

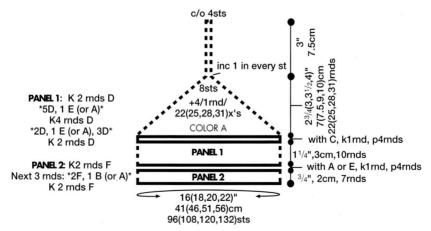

Merci

■ Everyone always asks me how I do it all, and the truth is that it would be impossible without my gifted, extraordinarily talented team! A book like this one is an enormous endeavor above and beyond the design. Produc-

Isabel Smiles with model Katherine

tion for this book took an entire year, a wild and wooly swirl of creative energy—schedul-ing and scouting talent and locations, orga-nizing photo shoots and finding props, then rescheduling the whole kit and caboodle when kids were sick at the last minute, shop-ping for the perfect elusive size 2 accessory, making panicked phone calls for a stand-in model for a no-show . . . it all continued for months! The truth is that if I knit for a hun-dred days I could never catch up with my merry band of knitters, could never even begin to write patterns with the clarity, simplicity, and accuracy of Carla Scott. I could never, even on a clear and sparkling day with perfect light and angelic children, ever begin to capture the antics and charisma of my models as Nina Fuller does. I could never charm a child, curl the hair, and fix the innumerable,

Nina Fuller with her son, Spencer, and daughter, Lily—both models!

infinitesimal details that catch the eye of my stylist, Merle Hagelin. And as for sets—I will admit to some ideas, but as the French say, *oh là là* . . . Isabel Smiles. So yes, I do it all, but I never do it alone!

Merle Hagelin with granddaughter Erica

Learn-to-Knit Puppet, Olivia Hendry
La Bébé, Sidney Ann Heath
Spring Coat and Pillbox Hat, Erica Joyce
Bellissima, Hannah Milam
Brittany Jumper, McDonough Scanlon
Tyrolean Waistcoat, Hunter Scanlon and Logan Gress Marshall
Sweet Pea, Mary Elizabeth Badger and Eva Light
Zigzag, Lily Hoffman
Swedish Day Dress, Brianna Lindsay
Beach Robe, Zachary Kaplan
Sunsuit, Meghan Clifford
Au Bateau, Luke Ford
Bow Wow, Hannah Milam and Caroline Jiang Bulger
School Days, Fritz Madrell and Elle Davies
Button, Button, Eleanor MacKenzie and Meghan Clifford
Hum Bug, Jamie Moore
One-Button Vest, Olivia Hendry
Twirl, Lorenza Lattanzi
Tutti Frutti, Eva Light and Abigail Menard
Jailbird, Dylan Henry-Tingle and Emma Stehli
Denim Bibs, Caleb Eliot Grant and Tucker Troast
Parka, Katherine Whitaker
Popcorn, Fritz Genner and Fiona Harbert
Snowflake, Katherine Whitaker and Stephanie Gallagher
Aran Pull, Spencer Hoffman and Lily Hoffman
Twizzle Tops, Olivia Hendry and Lily Hoffman

■ Other enormous thanks go to my literary agent, Sandy Taylor; to my patient and esteemed editor, Lauren Shakely; to Susan DeStaebler for her extraordinary graphic design talents; to Andrea Connolly Peabbles and Joy Sikorski for their fine production editorial and managerial skills; to my

mother, Nancy Whipple Lord, for teaching me how to knit; and to my grandmother Flora Whipple for teaching *her* to knit. Thanks to Penelope Coit for witty and accurate proofreading. Thanks to Mary Milam, my knitting master and eagle-eyed pattern checker. Thanks to Judith Shangold for incredible support and encouragement from the very beginning. Thanks to June and Ken Bridgewater at Westminster Fibers, and to inspirational Stephen Sheard, the creator of Rowan Yarns International, for, oh, such beautiful yarns and colors!

And once again, last but not least, special thanks to Cos Lattanzi, who was my business partner for many years.

To everyone, bravo and merci!

From My Bookshelf

■ Books on knitting abound, but I have found a few to be particularly wonderful—full of insight, technical information, and design inspiration.

Editors of Vogue Knitting, *Vogue Knitting.* New York, Pantheon Books, 1989. *One of my favorites, this book is rich in history and great for technique, with clear illustrations for just about everything. It is required for my classes, and has good basic design information and some traditional patterns.*

Goldberg, Rhoda Ochser. *The New Knitting Dictionary.* New York, Crown Publishers, 1984.

Hiatt, June Hemons. *The Principles of Knitting.* New York, Simon and Schuster, 1988.

Newton, Deborah. *Designing Knitwear.* Taunton Press, 1992. *A fabulous book on design, including history, technique, and new ways to see.*

Norbury, James, and Margaret Aguter. *Old-hams Encyclopedia of Knitting.* London, Oldham's Books, Ltd., 1957.

Square, Vicki. *The Knitter's Companion.* Interweave Press, 1996. *Tuck this into your knitting bag for a quick, convenient reference book.*

Standfield, Lesley. *The New Knitting Stitch Library.* Chilton Book Company, 1992. *Comprehensive, with some new stitches for inspiration.*

Stanley, Montse. *The Handknitter's Handbook.* London: David and Charles, 1986. *Great source for various cast-on techniques.*

Zimmerman, Elizabeth. *Knitter's Almanac.* Charles Scribner's Sons, 1974. Reprint, New York: Dover Publications, 1981.

———. *Knitting Without Tears.* New York: Charles Scribner's Sons, 1971.

In Short

approx	approximately
beg	begin(ning)
CC	contrasting color
ch	chain
cn	cable needle
cont(s)	continu(e) (ing) (s)
dec	decrease(s)
DK	double knitting yarn
dpn	double-pointed needle(s)
est	established
foll	follow(s) (ing)
inc(s)	increase(s)
k	knit
k2tog	knit two stitches together
LH	left-hand
lp(s)	loop(s)
MC	main color
p	purl
p2tog	purl two stitches together

pat(s)	pattern(s)
psso	pass the slipped stitch over the last stitch worked
rem	remain(ing) (s)
rep	repeat(s)
rev	reverse
RH	right-hand
rnd(s)	round(s) in circular knitting
RS	right side
sc	single crochet
sl	slip(ped) (ping). Slip stitches from left-hand needle to right-hand needle without knitting.
St st	stockinette stitch
st(s)	stitch(es)
tog	together
WS	wrong side
yo	yarn over

Needle Conversions

Metric	US	Old UK	Metric	US	Old UK
2 mm	0	14	5 mm	8	6
2¼ mm	1	13	5½ mm	9	5
2½ mm			6 mm	10	4
2¾ mm	2	12	6½ mm	10½	3
3 mm			7 mm		2
3¼ mm	3	10	7½ mm		1
3½ mm	4		8 mm	11	0
3¾ mm	5		9 mm	13	00
4 mm	6	8	10 mm	15	000
4½ mm	7	7			

Shopping Notes

■ The garments in this book have been knit in Rowan's beautiful yarns, as well as in a few others, including double knitting cotton, double knitting wool, worsted, bulky wool, kid silk mohair, and bulky cotton chenille. As always, we have listed both the yards and meters necessary for each garment, for your convenience. The incredibly rich color palette of Rowan yarns offers a range that is unbeatable, and we have included the actual color numbers for the yarns used for photography. Rowan yarns are distributed internationally, and the distributors below can give you information about where to shop in your area. We also have kits available, done in Rowan yarns complete with all necessary accessories, including the Learn-to-Knit Puppet, Twizzle Tops, Tutti Frutti, and Jailbird, from Jil Eaton at the Westminster Collections in the United States and Canada, and through Rowan Yarns in the United Kingdom; please contact them for information on yarns and kits. I have also included various other suppliers who carry quite wonderful yarns.

Whatever yarns you choose, always buy the very best you can afford. When you're spending hours and hours working on a project, delicious yarns add to the joy of knitting, and will provide the lucky owner of the garment with years of enjoyment as well!

■ UNITED STATES
Westminster Fibers
5 Northern Boulevard
Amherst, NH 03031

■ GREAT BRITAIN
Rowan Yarns
Green Lane Mill
Holmfirth, West Yorkshire
HD7 1RW

■ AUSTRALIA
MacEwen Enterprises
1/178 Cherry Lane
Laverton North
Vic 3026

■ BELGIUM
Hedera
Pleinstraat 68
3001 Leuven

■ CANADA
MINNOWKNITS™ Patterns
S.R. Kertzer
105A Winges Road
Woodbridge, Ontario
L4L 6C2

Rowan Yarns
Diamond Yarn
9697 St. Laurent
Montreal, Quebec
H3L 2N1

■ DENMARK
Filcolana A/S
Hagemannsvej 26–28
DK 8600 Silkeborg

■ FRANCE
Elle Tricote
52 rue Principale
67300 Schiltigheim

■ GERMANY
Wolle & Design
Wolfshovener Strassa 76
522428 Julich-Stetternich

■ HOLLAND
Henk & Henrietta Beukers
Dorpstraat 9
5327 AR Hurwenen

■ HONG KONG
Cheer Wool Co.
4 Fenwick Street
Wan Chai

■ ICELAND
Storkurinn
Kjorgardi
Laugavegi 59
ICE-101 Reykjavik

■ JAPAN
Dia Keito Co Ltd.
2-3-11 Senba Higashi
Minoh City
Osaka 562

■ NEW ZEALAND
MacEwen Enterprises
24b Allright Place
Mt. Wellington
Auckland

■ NORWAY
Eureka
PO Box 357
1401-Ski

■ SWEDEN
Wincent
Sveavagen 94
113 50 Stockholm

■ OTHER SUPPLIERS
Addi Turbo Needles
Skacel Collection, Inc.
224 SW 12th Street
Renton, WA 98055

Classic Elite Yarns
12 Perkins Street
Lowell, MA 10854

Cynthia Helene Yarns
Unique Kolours
1428 Oak Lane
Downington, PA 19335

Index